The Simple Pattern

A Straight-Forward Explanation of Institutionalism & Related Issues

JIM DEASON

General Editor

Scripture quotations marked "**NKJV**" taken from the *New King James Version*. Copyright 1979, 1980, 1982 by Thomas Nelson, inc. Used by permission. All rights reserved.

Scripture quotations marked "**NASB**" taken from the *New American Standard Bible: 1995 Update*. LaHabra, CA: The Lockman Foundation, 1995.

Scripture Quotations marked "**ESV**" taken from *The Holy Bible: English Standard Version*. Wheaton: Standard Bible Society, 2001.

Scripture quotations marked "**KJV**" taken from *The Holy Bible: King James Version*.

Scripture quotations marked "**ASV**" were taken from the *American Standard Version*. 1901 edition.

The contributors, editor, and others responsible for the production of this book have taken great care to accurately cite all other works referred to throughout this book whenever such information was available. If errors are found or information is lacking, write to book@eciconference.com, providing the location within the book and correct information, and the information will be updated in subsequent editions.

DEDICATED TO...

...the men who lived through the institutional division and, because of their dedication to truth, stood their ground. They preached the simple New Testament pattern regarding the work and organization of the church in spite of ridicule and attempts to muffle their voices by quarantine. Their meetings were canceled, pulpits were closed to them, certain papers refused to print their articles, but they pressed on and set our feet on higher ground. God bless their memory.

ACKNOWLEDGMENTS

I could never have produced this work without the help of three very special young preachers. Phillip Shumake used his incredible graphic abilities to design the cover and offered valuable insight into the publication process. Heath Robertson prepared the manuscripts for publication and helped with the editing. David Deason was the one who came up with the idea for this book in the first place, and helped finance the project. One would be hard pressed to find three more dedicated, faithful, and talented young preachers anywhere. I owe you each a debt I cannot repay.

Jim Deason

Today, at least two different groups have emerged with little or no fellowship existing between them. However one chooses to describe these groups—whether liberal or conservative, institutional or non-institutional—the chasm is wide and the differences continue to multiply. This book is about these issues.

The contributors to this study are well known among brethren. Steve Wolfgang and Dan King are outstanding in their respective fields—Steve as an historian and Dan as a scholar. Their work in this book will speak for itself. Paul Earnhart, L. A. Stauffer, Carroll Sutton, and Bill Hall are older preachers this editor has long admired for their years of faithful service to our King. They lived the division. They felt the pain of ruptured relationships because of their stand for the truth. When I think of these men, I am reminded of the financial commercial that once said, "When E. F. Hutton speaks, people listen." Well, I don't know about Hutton; you don't hear much from them anymore. I do, however, know something of these men. We need to listen.

I pray that you will read this book with profit and pass it along to others who might likewise benefit.

In His Kingdom,

Jim Deason
General Editor

1

HISTORY AND BACKGROUND OF
THE INSTITUTIONAL CONTROVERSY

STEVE WOLFGANG

"While there are a few places where 'anti-ism' is still a real
threat to the true faith, it is generally of no consequence.
Isolated little groups of 'antis' still meet; but they are withering
away and are having no appreciable effect on the brotherhood
at large." This analysis of the dreaded "antis," written by a
young preacher at the end of the1960s, probably summarized
the "majority view" in Churches of Christ toward "non-
cooperation" churches. This "false doctrine" was not only
labeled "antagonistic to clear Bible teaching" but the typical
"anti usually cut his own throat by his arrogant and malicious
acts and statements" and was "quick to draw a line of
fellowship and exclude himself from the larger portion of our

brotherhood." [1]

A decade later, the editor of the **Gospel Advocate** reiterated the "dying-on-the-vine" theme in an editorial in which he estimated that the "antis" composed 5 percent of churches of Christ and pleaded with them to "come back home . . . to the old paths . . . and preach again in the great churches," alleging that "anti doctrine cannot build great churches, inspire missionaries, and encourage pure and undefiled religion." [2] A well-known church-supported-college professor argued not long afterward that those who teach that Christians could "visit fatherless and widows by taking them in your home" have "taken the narrow, crooked pig-path of radicalism." [3]

Such comments were typical of a long train of caustic rhetoric that had continued for decades, including this fine example: "Infidelity, agnosticism, and 'anti-ism' have much in common. None ever brought a helping hand or healing ministry to the unfortunate of earth living in want and misery. Nor have they ever built a home for homeless children or a hospital in which to minister to the sick." [4]

As one might expect, such florid rhetoric was occasionally answered in like manner. One young preacher, describing a college lectureship which included at least four sessions of what can only be described "anti bashing," accused those who made a hobby of being anti-anti of having a "denominational concept of Christianity" and "a blind spot with regard to

---

1 Rubel Shelley, "Some Basic Errors of Liberalism," in *The Church Faces Liberalism: Freed-Hardeman College Lectures, 1970* (Nashville: Gospel Advocate Company, 1970), pp. 33-34. I have "heard through the grapevine" that the author of these disparaging remarks has lived to regret them, and while I can appreciate that sentiment, these comments have never, to my knowledge, been retracted or amended, nor, despite a recent outbreak of public apologies for various sins of the past, has anything similar occurred with reference to these and many other such allegations

2 Ira North, "Our Anti-Cooperation Brethren Should Come Back Home," *Gospel Advocate*, 121:19 (May 10, 1979), pp. 290,294.

3 Tom Holland, *Challenge of the Commission: Sermon Outlines from Acts* (Brentwood, TN: Penman Press, 1980), p. 20.

4 Gayle Oler, "No Soup," *Boles Home News*, March 25, 1954, p. 1

establishing authority regarding matters which divide us."
Other assessments of the "liberals" have included descriptions
ranging from "ignorant" to "deluded" to "malicious." [5]

How did it come to this? What produced such rhetoric, and the
divisive actions which often accompanied it? In this paper, I
propose to do several things:

(1) Sketch a brief historical account of the events which elicited
the comments just quoted. I intend for this section to be
history, fairly told, rather than propaganda, bringing whatever
historical training and ability I may possess to those ends.
Most historians long ago abandoned any illusions of being
totally "objective," but like most, I want to be fair. Like
everyone else, I have a viewpoint which despite my best efforts
will occasionally bob to the surface, and fairness and honesty
as a historian impel me to recognize it rather than hiding
behind the fictional mask of "objectivity."

I believe that the record will demonstrate that this division was
not one-sided, as it so often has been portrayed – blamed on a
bunch of cantankerous nuts who couldn't think straight,
wanted to be big fish in a small pond, or were just plain mean.
One surely might find examples of all of the above, but such
generalizations simply will not float as historical explanation.
Should I seem to fail in my attempt to be fair and even-handed,
I would be open to corrections.

(2) In my role as a historian, I report the results of a survey
questionnaire sent to more than 100 preachers, elders, and
members of "conservative" or "non-institutional" churches of
Christ, as a part of the preparation for the Nashville Meeting
in 1988. I make no claims for it as a scientific polling device,
but I did try to circulate it among what I perceive to be a
typical, or representative, sampling of those then living and
with personal memories of the events which caused them to

---

5 Steve Wolfgang, "Do You Have Time?" *Weekly Reminder* 15:21 (February 9,
1977), pp. 1-2 (Expressway Church of Christ, Louisville, KY). See also Wolfgang
exchange of letters with William Woodson, *ibid.*, 15:39 (June 15, 1977) pp. 2-3. Other
comments from questionnaires returned to the author in October-November, 1988.

oppose centralization of churches and church support of human institutions. More than 50completed questionnaires were returned, and I draw on the comments of several of them where they are germane to the discussion, seeking to answer at least part of the question, "How do we view each other?" The answers provided in these questionnaires are candid (in exchange for which I promised anonymity), and they are perhaps not always objective, but they express feelings honestly held. Some might question the accuracy of the perceptions they reveal, but the expressions of their views may help us as we seek to understand each other.

(3) I sometimes tire of the attempt to be "objective," and thus the third thing I wish to attempt is some sort of analysis of all this information in an attempt to answer not only "what happened" or "how," but "why." Some may not like what I say, and one is surely free to reject it if he wishes. All I ask is a fair hearing, without being dismissed out of hand.

Century of Progress?

Return with us now to those thrilling days of yesteryear – the prime time of N.B. Hardeman, G.C. Brewer, and Foy E. Wallace, Jr.; of Daniel Sommer, J.D. Tant and Joe Warlick; of H. Leo Boles, James A. Allen, and a cast of thousands. By all accounts, both the economic prosperity of the 1920s and the Depression of the 1930s were years of solid growth and development among churches of Christ. Although it is impossible to gather precise numerical data, the Census of Religious Bodies for 1926 reported more than 433,000 members for churches of Christ; several reliable sources estimated their numerical strength at upwards of half a million. [6] Not only were they growing numerically, but the gospel was spreading geographically, across what a later generation would dub the "Sunbelt," and into the "Rustbelt" of the industrial North, into

---

6 U.S. Bureau of Census . . . *Religious Bodies, 1926*. Washington, D.C., 1930,11, 394, 396; see H. Leo Boles, "Query Department," *Gospel Advocate* 69 (January 20, 1927), 62; G.A. Dunn, "Brother Batsell Baxter's School," *Firm Foundation* 42:30 (July 28, 1925), p. 3; John Allen Hudson, "New Census Incomplete," *Gospel Advocate* 82:50 (December 12, 1940), 1180.

places like Chicago, Detroit, Indianapolis, Cincinnati, Pittsburg, Philadelphia, Los Angeles and the West Coast.[7]

Institutionally and educationally, various parachurch organizations were also growing and prospering. Nashville Bible School had become David Lipscomb College, and Harding College settled in Searcy, Arkansas in 1934 after sojourning awhile in Bowling Green, KY, Odessa, MO, Cordell, OK, Harper, KS, and Morrillton, AR.[8] When George Pepperdine college joined the ranks of these and other schools such as Abilene Christian and Freed-Hardeman College a band of colleges stretching from Tennessee through Texas to the West Coast was completed.[9] Orphanages, beginning with Tennessee Orphan Home in 1909, included other institutional orphan care facilities such as Potter Orphanage (Bowling Green, KY, 1914), Boles Home (Quinlan, TX, 1927), and Tipton (Tipton, OK, 1928).[10]

---

7 For a general history of this period see Earl West, *Search For the Ancient Order*, IV, 1987. Themes in this paragraph are developed more specifically in Steve Wolfgang, "Myths and Realities: Churches of Christ in the Twentieth Century" (paper read at the Restoration History Conference, Bethany College, July 1977); and Wolfgang, "From Dissent to Consent: Twentieth Century Churches of Christ" (paper read at the American Society Church History Meeting, Southwest Missouri State University, Springfield, March 1979).

8 For an account of the Harding/Armstrong cluster of colleges, see Lloyd Cline Sears, *For Freedom. The Biography of John Nelson Armstrong* (Austin, TX: Sweet Publishing Company, 1969).

9 See M. Norvel Young, *A History of Christian Colleges Established and Controlled by Members of the Churches of Christ* (Kansas City, MO: Old Paths Book Club, 1949) for a history of the growth and development of various schools and colleges. The relationship of colleges and churches is also discussed in David Edwin Harrell, Jr., *Churches of Christ in the Twentieth Century: Homer Hailey's Personal Journey of Faith* (Tuscaloosa: University of Alabama Press, 2000), pp.

10 On Potter Orphanage, see Ben F. Taylor, *History of Potter Orphan Home* (Bowling Green, KY: Potter Orphan Home and School, n.d.). For related developments see "Christian Colleges" and "Education and Benevolence" (Chapter 9 and 10) in Earl West, *Search for the Ancient Order, III*, pp. 234-304. An example of a typical appeal on behalf of an orphanage can be found in *Childhaven News* 1:6 (October 1949), pp. 1,4. Abuses at this particular home have been featured prominently in the secular press as well as various papers reflecting the non-institutional position. See *Birmingham News*, Sunday April 22,1984, pp. IA, 10A; Ken Green, "The Childhaven Affair," *Searching the Scriptures* 25:9 (September 1984), pp. 197-201, which featured an interview with a preacher who lived at Childhaven from 19631972 while a child. See also Jack Holt Jr., "Victims of Institutionalism," *Gospel Anchor* 10:2 (October 1983), pp. 28-31.

New technologies such as radio, the automobile and the infant airline industry allowed rapid and widespread dissemination of the gospel. So frequently was the gospel heard on WLAC in Nashville that the station was dubbed, "We Love All Campbellites." Wide-area broadcasts such as the one on KRLD in Dallas shared by two young preachers and law-school students, W.L. Oliphant and Roy E. Cogdill, were commonplace.[11]

It was also, arguably, a period marked generally by doctrinal harmony and unity. Although it would be difficult to get the entire cast of preachers named above to agree on every issue, and while it is true that strong egos resulted in various frictions, by and large the period since the division of Churches of Christ and Christian Churches until World War II was primarily one of significant doctrinal harmony. Even the few instances of disagreement prove the rule: those who deviated could be expected to be, and were, roasted as heretics.[12]

Even the most vocal and visible divisive issue, premillennialism, serves as an illustration of the relative doctrinal unanimity among the churches. Although the issue created quite a disturbance (seemingly as much because some did not criticize it extensively enough to satisfy its most vocal opponents as for the specific issue itself), the number of churches actually espousing the doctrine was quite limited. By and large, it was effectively contained in a small number of churches localized in Kentucky, Indiana, and Louisiana – churches which a generation later numbered only about 100 with perhaps 10,000 members. The quickest and most effective way to tar a church or college in the 1930s was to label them

---

11 "Our Messages" (from E. A. Timmons, M.D., Columbia, TN), Gospel Advocate 69:1 (January 6, 1927), p. 8; see William S. Banowsky, *The Mirror of a Movement: Churches of Christ as Seen Through the Abilene Christian College Lectureship* (Dallas: Christian Publishing Company, 1965), p. 319.

12 Several of the themes introduced in this paragraph are explored in detail in Richard T. Hughes, *Reviving the Ancient Faith: The Story of Churches of Christ in America* (Grand Rapids, MI: William B. Eerdmans Publishing Company, 1996). For yet another differing perspective, see Thomas H. Olbricht, *Hearing God's Voice: My Life With Scripture in the Churches of Christ* (Abilene, TX: ACU Press, 1996).

"premillennial sympathizers." [13]

Perhaps a portion of this relative internal harmony can be seen in the numerous widely-publicized and well attended debates during the period. N.B. Hardeman's debates on instrumental music with Ira Boswell of the Christian church and with the well-known Baptist Ben Bogard; G.C. Brewer's discussion with "companionate marriage" advocate Judge Ben Lindsey; Foy E. Wallace's skirmish with Texas Fundamentalist J. Frank Norris, and a host of others literally too numerous to mention, revealed a remarkable unanimity in the church on fundamental issues, as well as a manifest militance against all perceived threats to the faith. Certainly, to their religious neighbors, the church surely looked like a coherent, united, militant and growing religious body.[14]

"Unity efforts" of a sort were underway as well. When Daniel Sommer, estranged for thirty years from his co-belligerents in the instrument/missionary society controversy, embarked in 1933 on an extended tour of the South, his visits to Nashville, Henderson, Memphis, Dallas, and other places resulted in significantly decreased tensions over the right of colleges to exist and of churches to employ local evangelists and use Bible class literature. The failure of his alliance with F.D. Kershner of the Christian Church to promote harmony between the two groups may have given impetus to the Witty-Murch "unity meetings" of the next decade, but also reminds us that churches of Christ were largely united in rejecting such

---

13 Steve Wolfgang, "The Impact of Premillennialism on the Church," *Guardian of Truth* 30:1 (January 2, 1986), pp. 1315, 29; Cecil Willis, *W. W. Otey. Contender for the Faith* (Akron, OH: by the author, 1964), pp. 264-267, 304, 310312; William Woodson, *Standing for Their Faith: A History of churches of Christ in Tennessee, 1900-1950* (Henderson, TN: J&W Publications, 1979), chapter 11; and Banowsky, pp. 196-199, 223-224.

14 The relationship between churches of Christ and other religious bodies is explored in Wolfgang, "Churches of Christ and the Fundamentalist Controversy" (paper read at the American Academy of Religion meeting, Atlanta, GA, 1981); see also James Stephen Wolfgang, *Fundamentalism and Churches of Christ* (M.A. thesis, Vanderbilt University, 1990).

overtures.[15]

In summary, when one looks at churches of Christ in the mid-20th century, one can easily make a case, at least on the surface, for a high level of doctrinal unity and harmony; an agreement on the spiritual nature and work of the church, and the kind of distinctive, no-nonsense preaching which was common knowledge both among members of the church and their religious neighbors.

One need not be an "anti" to have such perceptions; several historians among institutional churches state the obvious: "There was a time when Churches of Christ were widely known as a people of the Book. All who knew us knew that we hungered above all for the word of God. They knew that we immersed ourselves in its truths and sacrificed dearly to share the gospel with those who had never heard. These were our most fundamental commitments. We knew it, and others knew it." Although these authors disdainfully reject "the hard and ugly sectarian spirit which did incalculable damage to our movement for so many years," they make a strong case for the invasion of secularism as "American members of Churches of Christ have spiraled upward to a much higher socio-economic plane." While I reject the solution they propose, and their pejorative use of terms such as "rigid, dogmatic, sectarian spirit" which produced a "posture of aloofness," I believe they are substantially correct in their analysis of the present, if not their representation of the past or their proposals for the future.[16]

---

15 See James Stephen Wolfgang, "Daniel Sommer," in *The Encyclopedia of the Stone-Campbell Movement* [hereinafter *ESCM*] (Grand Rapids, MI: William B. Eerdmans Publishing Company, 2004), pp. 692-694. See also Steve Wolfgang, "Controversy Concerning Unity Movements Among Churches of Christ" in *Their Works Do Follow Them: Florida College Annual Lectures, 1982* (Tampa, FL: Florida College, 1982), pp. 213-239; Wolfgang, "Consequences of Factionalism,"" in *Factionalism: A Threat to the Church* (Fairmount, IN: Guardian of Truth Foundation, 1983), pp. 90-96. Both are based on James Stephen Wolfgang, *A Life of Humble Fear: The Biography of Daniel Sommer, 1850-1940* (M.A. thesis, Butler University, 1975).

16 C . Leonard Allen, Richard T. Hughes, and Michael R. Weed, *The Worldly Church: A Call For Biblical. Renewal* (Abilene, TX:ACU Press, 1988). Quotations are from pp. 1-2, 6-7.

Two recollections by well-known older preachers who began preaching in those days well summarize the case. When asked to compare the church and its members in the 1980s to those of the 1930s, a former president of David Lipscomb College responded, "I don't think they see the glory of the church, unencumbered by denominationalism, as I did . . . when I was growing up." Furthermore, he opined, "I don't think members of the church think the church is different from Protestantism. When I started preaching members of the church believed Protestants needed to be saved. We've lost a lot of that. It goes back to an understanding of the distinctiveness of the church. At an earlier time they really felt the gospel was a lot better than Protestantism."[17]

These sentiments are echoed succinctly by G.K. Wallace, describing his earliest preaching days in the 1920s and 1930s: "Most of the baptisms were from the denominations. In those days denominational people would come to our meetings. . . . Denominational people do not come these days to our meetings and if they did they would not, in most places, hear anything that would lead them out of false doctrine."[18]

But other forces and factors were at work, as well, as the following summary by Bill Humble well illustrates: "larger and more expensive buildings, the more affluent middle-class membership, the number of full-time ministers, the increasing emphasis on Bible schools and Christian education, and missionary outreach all reflect a gradual but impressive growth. . . . After World War II the church enjoyed a remarkable growth in urban areas. As its members climbed the economic and educational ladder, the church moved 'across the tracks.'"[19]

---

17 Robert E. Hooper and Jim Turner, *Willard Collins, The People Person* (Nashville: 20th Century Christian, 1986), pp. 116, 118.

18 G.K. Wallace, *Autobiography and Retirement Sermons* (High Springs, FL: Mary Lois Forrester, 1983), p. 17.

19 Bill Humble, *The Story of the Restoration* (Austin, TX: Firm Foundation, 1969), p. 70. See James Marvin Powell and M. Norvel Young, *The Church is Building* (Nashville: Gospel Advocate, 1956). The "on-the-march" impulse to literally put

While I concur that World War II was a watershed in the history of churches of Christ, even before Pearl Harbor there were harbingers of what was to come. Although several colleges unobtrusively had been accepting contributions from church treasuries for years, G.C. Brewer created quite a stir at the 1938 ACC lectures when "many who were present understood Brewer to say that the church that did not have Abilene Christian College in its budget had the wrong preacher."[20] A decade later, N.B. Hardeman and others would revive this controversy in a public attempt to attract financial support for colleges directly from church treasuries.[21]

World War II

In truth, although there were such previews of what was to come, World War II can be seen as a chronological line of demarcation. First, as one generation passed from the earth, another was coming to prominence. In one eighteen month

---

Churches of Christ "on the map" by building new church buildings is analyzed in Richard Hughes, "Symbols of Modernization: The Institutional Church Building," in *Reviving the Ancient Faith*, pp. 244-253 and *passim*.

20 Willis, *W. W. Otey*, 287. See also Athens Clay Pullias, *Information Concerning Financial Gifts to David Lipscomb College by Congregations of the Church of Christ, 1891-1968* (Nashville, privately published [DLC?], n.d. [1968?]).

21 N.B. Hardeman, "Spending the Lord's Money," *Gospel Advocate* 92 (May 29, 1947), p. 372, and "The Banner Boys Become Enraged," *Firm Foundation* 64:43 (October 28, 1947), p. 1; Foy E. Wallace, Jr., *Bible Banner*, September, 1947, p. 16; Wolfgang, "Unity Movements," pp. 220-21, 234; Willis, W. W. Otey, pp. 321 ff.; on Hardeman, see J.M. Powell and Mary Nelle Hardernan Powers, *NBH: A Biography of Nicholas Brodie Hardeman* (Nashville: Gospel Advocate Company, 1964); and James R. Cope, "N.B. Hardeman: Orator, Evangelist, Educator, and Debater," in *They Being Dead Yet Speak: Florida College Annual Lectures, 1981* (Temple Terrace, FL: Florida College, 1981), pp. 133ff.

The argument advanced by Hardeman that the orphanage and the college "stand or fall together" would be championed more successfully fifteen years later (to a more receptive audience) by Batsell Barrett Baxter, *Questions and Issues of the Day in the Light of the Scriptures* (Nashville, 1963), and reviewed by James R. Cope, *Where Is The Scripture?* (Temple Terrace, FL: by the author), 1964; and James P. Needham, *A Review of Batsell Barrett Baxter's Tract: "May the Church Scripturally Support a College?"* (Orlando, FL: Truth Magazine Bookstore [reprint], 1970). Another advocate of church support of colleges, and a discussion of other related issues, is J.D. Thomas, *We Be Brethren: A Study in Biblical Interpretation* (Abilene, TX: Biblical Research Press, 1958). pp. 186-194.

period during 1940-41, as the nation prepared for war, a number of well-known older preachers (Daniel Sommer, J.D. Tant, Joe Warlick, F.B. Srygley – household names in many places in the brotherhood) passed away, and were "replaced" in positions of editorial responsibility by much younger men such as B.C. Goodpasture.[22]

Reactions to the war itself, and the discussion of the "carnal warfare" question revealed that an interesting shift of opinion had occurred between the wars as this new generation had come to prominence. As late as World War I, David Lipscomb's strong non-participatory stance still held sway among a strong and vocal minority in the church. Objections to Christians serving in war resulted in such incidents as the closing of Cordell Christian College by the local "defense council," and the arrest and threatened execution of two young Christians who were shipped to Leavenworth Prison, and lined up before a firing squad to be shot.[23] The Gospel Advocate ceased the re-publication of David Lipscomb's old articles on "Civil Government" and no-participation in warfare only under threat from federal government either to cease and desist the publication of such anti-war propaganda or be shut down altogether.[24]

---

22 Ed Harrell, "B.C. Goodpasture: Leader of Institutional Thought," in *They Being Dead Yet Speak: Florida College Annual Lectures, 1981* (Tampa: Florida College, 1981). Note Harrell's observations that "Foy Wallace scorched heretics; Goodpasture warned them that they would lose their position in the brotherhood" (p. 250). A recent full-length study of Goodpasture;s life and influence is John C. Hardin, *Common Cause: B.C. Goodpasture, the Gospel Advocate, and Churches of Christ in the Twentieth Century* (Ph.D. dissertation, Auburn University, 2004), accessible at "http://etd.auburn.edu/etd/bitstream/handle/10415/1682/Hardin2009.pdf?sequence=1". See also J.C. Choate, *The Anchor That Holds: The Life of Benton Cordell Goodpasture* (Nashville: Gospel Advocate Company, 1971).

23 Sears, *For Freedom*, pp. 156-157. The history of the pacifistic strain of thought in Restoration History is sketched in Michael Casey, "Pacifism," in *ESCM*, pp. 586-588.

24 Earl West, "World War I and the Decline of David Lipscomb's Civil Government" (unpublished ms., Harding Graduate School of Religion Library, 1976, p. 11); see West, III, chapter 13. For background on Lipscomb and nineteenth century pacifism, See David Edwin Harrell, Jr., "Disciples of Christ Pacifism in Nineteenth Century Tennessee," *Tennessee Historical Quarterly* 21:3 (September, 1962), pp. 263-274.

By World War II, however, shifting sentiment, the emergence of a new generation, and, to be sure, the surge of patriotic opinion following the attack on Pearl Harbor, produced a strikingly different environment. B.C. Goodpasture needed no government intervention to persuade him to close the columns of the Gospel Advocate to further discussion; by 1943 he did it voluntarily. Indeed, a close examination of some of the early criticisms of the cooperative efforts in preaching in Italy and Germany stemmed from the fact that some of the "missionaries" seemed to their critics much too quick to "apologize" for the devastation inflicted on Europe by American armed forces.[25]

The Post-World War II Era

Even before the army of GI's returned home in 1945 to marry, continue their education, or launch careers (or all of the above), a new consciousness regarding evangelism and a seeming willingness to try whatever sounded good in spreading the gospel had overtaken many of the churches and those who preached or served as elders over them. The educational boon of the GI Bill also swelled the ranks of colleges across the country – and "Christian colleges" seemed determined not to be a whit behind the chiefest.

Spurred in most cases, no doubt, by well-intentioned impulses to spread the gospel as widely as possible, churches were inundated after the war with numerous appeals: to support cooperative works in Germany, Italy, and Japan ("overseen" by churches in Texas and Tennessee who assumed a centralizing role in such support); or the proliferation of institutions soon swelled to more than thirty);[26] and not least by the "Christian"

---

25 Cled Wallace, "That Rock Fight in Italy," *Gospel Guardian* 1:36 (January 19,1950), pp. 1,5; Foy E. Wallace, Jr., ""Going Off Half-Cocked," *Gospel Guardian* 1:44 (March 16, 1950), pp. 1,5; Roy E. Cogdill, "We Are Not Anti-Foreign Evangelism," *Gospel Guardian* 1:47 (April 6, 1950), pp. 1,5. See Willis, *W. W. Otey*, pp. 306f.

26 Willis, *W. W. Otey*, p. 312. In 1949 there were 14 "Orphan Homes and Homes for the Aged" listed in G.H. P. Showalter and Leslie G. Thomas, comps., *Church Directory and List of Preachers of Churches of Christ* (Austin, TX: Firm Foundation Publishing House, 1949), p. 212).

colleges, whose swelling enrollments of returning GI's helped create a seemingly insatiable appetite for funds to sustain their growth.

That there had been some "historical precedent" for centralized support of city-wide evangelistic endeavors cannot be successfully disputed. The cooperative efforts of the Hardeman "Tabernacle Meeting" of the 1920's and 1930's were reflected in other such post-World II endeavors as the Houston Music Hall meetings, in which the Norhill church undertook to oversee funds from Houston-area churches so that Foy E. Wallace, Jr., could preach lessons which, transcribed and later published as *God's Prophetic Word* and *Bulwarks of the Faith*, would provide sermon material on which an entire generation of preachers would "cut their teeth." The local preachers at Norhill at that time were Luther Blackmon and Wallace's close friend, Roy E. Cogdill, who before long would launch his own printing company largely to be able to publish Wallace's books as well as his paper, the *Bible Banner* (later, the *Gospel Guardian* – in which Cogdill would later renounce the centralized arrangement of the Music Hall meeting).[27]

Cogdill, Blackmon, *Gospel Guardian* editor Yater Tant, and others who initially supported such efforts were forced by conviction of conscience, and, as they saw it, consistency, to withdraw their support for such collective endeavors in much the same way as men like Tolbert Fanning and Benjamin Franklin, initial supporters and defenders of nineteenth-century missionary society endeavors, eventually withdrew their support for such efforts and indeed became vocal opponents of such works.[28]

---

27 For a general summary of Cogdill's life and significance, see James Stephen Wolfgang, "Cogdill, Roy E. (1907-1985)," in ECSM, pp.225-226. For specific information referenced in the paragraph, see Cogdill and Guy N. Woods, *Cogdill-Woods Debate: A Discussion on what constitutes scriptural cooperation between churches of Christ* (Lufkin, TX: Gospel Guardian Company, n.d. [1958?], pp. 204-208, 214-215.

28 See James R. Wilburn, *The Hazard of the Die: Tolbert Fanning and the Restoration Movement* (Austin, TX Sweet Publishing Company, 1969, chapters 10-12, especially pp. 176-181, 187-188, 193-195; Earl West, *Elder Ben Franklin: Eye of the Storm* (Indianapolis: Religious Book Service, 1983), pp. 158-160, 211, 222ff.; Joseph

For those who began to think twice about centralized foreign evangelistic efforts "under the oversight" of a single large American church, an additional concern was the message preached (or, in the eyes of many, not preached) by the "missionaries" receiving such support. David Filbeck has ably demonstrated that much of the opposition to the centralized missionary society of the Christian Church was due to the diluted (even modernistic) message of those so supported, and some of the same concerns – as much about message as about methods – are, I believe, reflected in some of the writing in opposition to centralized evangelistic support, where many smaller churches contributed to support preachers in the countries devastated by World War II by sending their contributions to a large, prosperous, "overseeing" church.[29]

What Were "The Issues?"

The proliferation of humanly-arranged institutions seeking church contributions (particularly the increasing volume of educational institutions openly soliciting money from churches), and the growing numbers of congregations assuming the right to "oversee" the work of other churches with the financial support of many more, were only a part of the

---

Franklin and J.A. Headington, *The Life and Times of Benjamin Franklin* (St. Louis: John Burns, Publisher, 1879), pp. 304-305.

The discussion of "historical precedent" is an interesting one which one or both sides often adduce to bolster claims, but which is ultimately meaningless since, even were it uniform, what the "pioneers" did provides no validity for doctrine or practice unless one accepts an "authority of tradition" viewpoint akin to that of Roman Catholicism. In this context, it simply demonstrates that sincere, intelligent, and honorable persons can and do change their minds and actions for a variety of reasons; or, that people sometimes do contradictory things and are not always self-consistent.

29 David Filbeck, *The First Fifty Years: A Brief History of the Direct-Support Missionary Movement* (Joplin, MO: College Press Publishing Company, 1980), pp. 36-59. While the objections of some of the opponents of centralized missionary work among churches of Christ did not center around traditional "modernism," the heavy emphasis on the social gospel aspects of much "mission work" was a definite factor. See the articles cited in note 25 above, as well as Otis Gatewood, *Preaching in the Footsteps of Hitler* (Nashville: Williams Printing company, 1960), pp. 72-75. Though defending his "relief works" in Germany, Gatewood acknowledged that "Problems arose as a result of such work, it is true. Some wanted to be baptized only to get food and clothing." Furthermore, "all this [distribution of food and clothing] took much time that could have been spent teaching the Bible" (pp. 70, 72).

scenario. Combined with the upward socio-economic mobility of members of the church, many of whom experienced the shift from the day-to-day, hand-to-mouth existence of Depression-era poverty to the disposable income and consumerism of the post-war boom which moved the South toward parity with the nation, these factors and more provided a complex scenario fraught with possibilities for differences, disagreement, and division.[30]

By the time a national radio (and later, television) program, the "Herald of Truth," was added to the list of orphanages, homes for the aged and for unwed mothers, schools, colleges, publishing ventures (Gospel Press, for example) and intermittent appeals for increasing numbers of projects centralized under a few large, prosperous churches, an increasing number of brethren began to question various aspects of these endeavors. The study of "the current issues" (as they were often generically labeled) produced a tension between the boosters of the new projects and those who raised pesky questions about their scriptural validity. That tension was reflected in the increasing vehemence with which both sides pressed their positions in various "brotherhood journals." Roy Cogdill's Banner Publishing Company was created in large part to allow Foy E. Wallace, Jr., to continue in the *Banner/Guardian* his opposition to the increasingly open appeals for church support of colleges, orphanages and other parachurch enterprises which surfaced with increasing frequency in B.C. Goodpasture's *Gospel Advocate* and in Texas *Firm Foundation* after G.H.P. Showalter was succeeded in 1954 by Reuel Lemmons.[31]

Other papers were begun as well, often for the expressed

---

30 For perceptive commentary on these intertwined doctrinal, social, economic, and other "issues," see Richard Hughes, chapter 10, "The Fight Over Modernization," in *Reviving the Ancient Faith*; see also Harrell, "Non-Institutional Movement," in *ESCM*, pp. 567-569.

31 Foy E. Wallace, Jr., Fanning Yater Tant, and Roy E. Cogdill, mimeographed letter, March 21, 1949; Foy E. Wallace, Jr., "The New Gospel Guardian," Fanning Yater Tant, "Policy of the Gospel Guardian," and Roy E. Cogdill, "Publisher's Statement," *Bible Banner* 12:3 (April 1949), 1-2.

purpose of examining these issues. *The Preceptor*, begun in 1951 by several brethren affiliated with Florida Christian College was followed almost a decade later by another Tampa journal, *Searching the Scriptures*. Midway between the launching of these journals, and half a continent away, *Truth Magazine* was begun in the Chicago area. None of these upstart journals, however, enjoyed the extended longevity and familiarity (to say nothing of the large subscription lists) of the *Gospel Advocate* and *Firm Foundation*, which were joined by new journals such as the Spiritual Sword in the flight against the "antis."[32]

The discussion of these "issues" was perhaps most vocally expressed in a series of formal debates in the half-decade beginning about. 1954. From Indianapolis (Holt-Totty, October 1954; Woods-Porter, January 1956) to Texas (Harper-Tant, Lufkin, April 1955 and Abilene, November 1955) to Alabama (Cogdill-Woods, Birmingham, November 1957; Wallace-Holt, Florence, December 1959), men who had once stood shoulder to shoulder and made common cause against all enemies now did battle with each other. These debates, published and re-published for wider consumption by various brotherhood printing concerns, reflected hundreds of other unpublished public discussions and thousands of private conversations and arguments which spread to nearly every hamlet in the land where there was a church of Christ. Together with the written discussions in various "brotherhood journals," they provided an arsenal for anyone who sought to do battle on either side.

---

32 Harrell reports that "by the early 1950's the *Advocate's* circulation had grown to over 20,000; during the centennial drive of 1954 and 1955, the number of subscribers rose to an inflated figure of over 100,000; by the time of Goodpasture's death in 1977, the circulation had stabilized at just over 30,000." Furthermore, he observes: "The *Gospel Advocate* was the most powerful single center of influence among the churches of Christ of the 1950s. Goodpasture formed strong alliances with other institutions, particularly David Lipscomb College. He was the outspoken friend of all the institutions supported by churches;. . . in return the leaders of those institutions promoted the *Advocate*" ("B.C. Goodpasture," in *Florida College Annual Lectures, 1981*, pp. 243, 249).

The Arguments

In debates, sermons, and various articles in religious journals, non-institutional preachers have normally advanced the following propositions:

1. That God has revealed in Scripture certain patterns for believers to follow in executing their collective duties in congregational work and worship (Heb. 8:5).

2. That these "binding" patterns are expressed in terms of (a) "generic" or "specific" statements or commands; (b) specific accounts of action, and (c) necessary conclusions or inferences drawn from Scripture (Acts 15).[33]

3. That the general or more "generic" statements or commands allow differing optional or expedient ways of obeying those requirements, while specific statements or examples provide more restrictive instructions and do not authorize alternative procedures.

4. That the differences between "general and specific" can be detected, and distinguished from incidentals, or from a variety of expedient ways, by correctly following common sense hermeneutical principles.[34]

---

33 See David Koltenbah, "The Three Methods of Argument to Establish Divine Authority and the Three Arguments in Acts 15 (Parts I-III)" *Truth Magazine* 11:10-12 (July, August, September, 1967), pp. 234ff., 255ff., 275ff.; "The Apostles' Appeal to Scriptural Authority," in *Biblical Authority, Its Meaning and Application: Florida College Annual Lectures, 1974* (Fairmount, IN: Cogdill Foundation, 1974), pp. 80-94. An M.A. thesis by Milo, Hadwin at Abilene Christian College which assails the idea that apostolic examples provide any basis of New Testament authority was published as *The Role of New Testament Examples as Related to Biblical Authority* (Austin, TX: Firm Foundation Publishing House, 1974). A conclusion, subtly stated on p. 53, is that there is no way to authorize observance of the Lord's Supper each first day of the week from the New Testament evidence (cf. pp. 39, 53). For alternate viewpoints, see Thomas B. Warren, *When Is An Example Binding?* (Jonesboro, AR: National Christian of Christ); "Why Are We at an Impasse?" *Restoration Quarterly* 30 (First Quarter 1988), pp. 17-42.

34 See Roy E. Cogdill, *Walking By Faith* (Lufkin: Gospel Guardian Company, 1957; 6th Ed., 1967), especially pp. 13-28; Earl West, "Learning a Lesson from History (no. 1-3)," *Gospel Guardian* 1:40, 41, 42 (February 16, 23 and March 2, 1950); and "Congregational Cooperation," *Gospel Guardian* 13:18 (September 7, 1961, pp. 273ff. [reprint]). For contrasting views, see Athens Clay Pullias, "Where There Is No

5. That the Scriptures enjoin upon Christians a broad range of individual duties, obligations and privileges which can be carried out in a variety of optional and expedient ways, that God may be glorified.

6. That, by contrast, the collective duties enjoined upon Christians in their collective congregational capacity, are fairly limited and consist of worshiping God through prayer, vocal music, proclamation of the gospel, and the first day of the week observance of the Lord's Supper and financial collection to enable the congregation to carry out its collective responsibilities in discharging its own edificational and teaching duties, assisting needy sanits, and supporting preachers in their work of proclamation and teaching.

7. That, while some collective duties may overlap individual obligations (teaching, singing, prayer, for example), individual and collective (congregational) activities are not identical and can be clearly distinguished one from the other.

8. That since collective activity, which requires a common mind, acceptance and agreement to common supervision (by elders, if qualified), and the pooling of financial resources, is inherently fraught with possibilities of disagreement in matters of detail, it should be limited to those activities clearly enjoined upon Christians in acting together as a congregation, allowing room to respect the conscience of others, even of weak or untaught brethren (Rom. 14).

9. That, in regard to preaching the gospel, Scripture reveals only that evangelism was accomplished by individual preachers, self-supported or remunerated by congregations (by example, directly, without the aid of some itermediary

Pattern," *Lipscomb Spring Lectures: Volume I* (Nashville: Gospel Advocate Company, 1954, pp. 90-102 (see Cecil N. Wright a lecture in the same volume [pp. 103-11.2], "Principles of New Testament congregational Cooperation," a summary of his series in the 1951 *Gospel Advocate*).

or "sponsoring" church, or "missionary society," whether called by that name or identified as a "steering committee" or other terminology – 2 Cor. 11:8-9; Phil. 4:15-18).

10. That Scripture several times records that churches assisted their own needy saints, or sent funds for the temporary relief of congregations in "want," – but that such relief was temporary, not sent from one prosperous church to another, and never for purposes of evangelism in which each congregation has equal obligations to the limit of its ability. Most conservatives have stressed the independence and autonomy of each local congregation, insisting that twentieth-century "sponsoring-church" conglomerates or other centralizing tendencies, no less than a missionary society or the Baptist associations and conventions, compromise New Testament principles regarding the nature of Christ's church.[35]

11. That the church Jesus died to purchase is a spiritual institution with a uniquely spiritual function, and is therefore not to be remade into a hybrid welfare organization-country club responsible for alleviating social ills or for the entertainment of its members.

12. That human societies and institutions (colleges, orphanages, publishing companies, hospitals, etc.) which may be utilized as expedient means on a fee-for-service basis, am not be appended to the church and maintain their livelihood by church donations, and that all such attempts to make them parachurch or church-related institutions is foreign to the New Testament.

---

[35] See Robert F. Turner, "Cooperation of Churches," in *The Arlington Meeting* (Orlando, FL: Cogdill Foundation, n.d. 1969]), pp. 252ff. This work is probably the most extensive and best discussion of the institutional "issues." See also Gaston D. Cogdell and Robert F. Turner, *The Cogdell- Turner Discussion* (Fairmount, IN: Guardian of Truth Foundation, 1983). On congregational independence, perhaps the clearest statement is Turner, "Restoration of Congregational Independence," in *The Restoration Heritage in America. A Biblical Appeal for Today*. Florida College Annual Lectures, 1976 (Marion, IN: Cogdill Foundation, 1976), pp. 213-229.

The Yellow Tag of Quarantine

Although discussions of these issues would persist and churches would continue to divide for at least another decade, by 1954 the editor of the *Gospel Advocate* was quite willing to entertain a motion that the "yellow tag of quarantine" (the stigma of which probably cannot be realized except by a generation which knew not antibiotics and the post-World War II "wonder drugs") be hung on the door of the infested "antis" in order to contain their contagion.[36]

In such an environment, the pressure on other institutions (particularly the newer schools such as Florida Christian College) to "go along" and "line up" could be resisted only at great risk to the financial health and "brotherhood prestige" (read: ability to attract tuition paying students and potential donors) of its administration and faculty. Business ventures (such as the CEI bookstore, for example) were openly boycotted if the positions of their owners and operators were considered heterodox.

Nor were the pressures any less on churches, many of which at least partially rationalized a $10 or $20 monthly orphanage donation on the grounds of "showing that we're not anti." Deacons and church treasurers who dared to reveal reservations about church support of institutions are known to have been told either to write a check to an institution or resign and go elsewhere.

For that matter, individual preachers, too many to be merely anecdotal, have reported cancellation of meetings, threats of termination of job or outside support ("if you espouse such a

---

36 B.C. Goodpasture, "An Elder Writes," *Gospel Advocate* 96:46 (November 18,1954, p. 906; and "They Commend the Elder Who Wrote," *Gospel Advocate* 96:49 (December 9, 1954), p. 962; Cecil B. Douthitt, "The Yellow Tag of Quarantine," *Gospel Guardian* 6:35 (January 13, 1955), p. 1. At the Dallas Meeting in July 1990, I was publicly challenged by some who alleged that this really did not happen, and since then in on-line discussions it has been alleged that this was not really a call for quarantine. One reason for citation is so such things can be checked, and so interested parties can read for themselves – which is something one should do before dogmatically denying or challenging a reference.

doctrine you won't have any place to preach") and occasional firings from local congregations because they dared to preach (or to preach against a majority view) on such controversial subjects. "Confessions" of wayward souls who repented, recanted, and were reclaimed from the heresy of "anti-ism" were featured prominently in the Gospel Advocate and included an impressive cast: Earl West, Pat Hardeman, Hugo McCord, C.M. Pullias, John D. Cox, and a host of others.[37]

The list goes on: "no anti need apply" in solicitations for preachers: "the closest thing to an anti church in the New Testament was 'Anti-och'"; fertilizer bags waved from the pulpit; "James 1:27" and/or "Galatians 6:10" printed in church ads and painted on church signs dotting the landscape. Lawsuits over property disputes, paraded across the pages of daily metropolitan newspapers for all the unbelieving world to see, while not commonplace, were not unknown.[38] Instances of fisticuffs and scuffles in the lobby were not uncommon. Carnality and ugliness abounded.

In short, by the early 1960's a clear message had been delivered to the minority tagged "anti" by the majority. Delivered with all the smug superiority and condescension of an older sibling, it said, "Go away, kid – you bother me." As Filbeck has demonstrated in his chronicle of the missionary society controversies,[39] a similar mentality had evolved which was no longer willing to consider optional many things originally defended as mere expediencies. The colleges, orphanages and other institutions appended to the churches now seemed to many to be indispensible – absolutely necessary – to the work of the church. Seen in this light, it was an easy

---

37 See, as merely one example, Earl West, "A Statement and an Explanation," *Gospel Advocate* September 19, 1957, p. 594, and other statements in succeeding issues over a period of several years.

38 See James P. Needham, *The Truth About the Trouble at Taylor Boulevard* (Louisville, KY, privately published, 1964). That the old "fertilizer-on-the-yard" argument was still alive and well, years after the division was accomplished, is readily apparent in Furman Kearley, "By All Means Save Some," *Gospel Advocate* 130:11 (November 1988), p. 5.

39 Filbeck, *The First Fifty Years*, 36-46.

step to elevate their value well above whatever questionable virtue the maintenance of fellowship with the cantankerous "antis" might possess. Noninstitutional brethren could be deemed expendable if they could not agree to go along and get along. Many in the "mainstream" churches seemed to believe their fellowship less valuable to the cause than the emerging network of colleges and other institutions erected and funded by the churches, ostensibly to the greater glory of God.

Without question, there may have been instances of non-institutional brethren who used "mirror logic," vacating the premises before they were invited to leave, displaying rancorous attitudes in the process, heaping derision and vilification upon their "liberal" opponents. I certainly am not suggesting that non-institutional brethren always behaved themselves as they should; surely there is enough sin to go around in this or any other division. Whatever the case, the division over institutionalism was clearly induced by much more fundamental causes than that some brethren on either side behaved themselves in a manner unbecoming to Christians – which is at least part of the reason why it will take more than simply "talking," or forming new friendships, to heal this breach. Division did not come simply because brethren mistreated each other – though no doubt some did – but was due to much more basic causes. It will not be reversed unless and until those more fundamental problems are remedied.

And whatever may be said of the conduct of individuals of either persuasion, it is certainly true that the levers of brotherhood "power" were clearly with the institutional majority, and the message they sent, perceived by their non-institutional brethren was a rough equivalent of "Go play in the traffic."

Separation, Growth and Development

And so they did. Despite the disdainful portrayals and reports of impending doom quoted at the beginning of this paper, "anti-ism" seems not to have perished from the earth just yet. Even while the controversy still raged in some places, historian Bill

Humble provided a clearer, more objective view of the situation: "The most serious issue that churches of Christ have faced in this century is church cooperation and 'institutionalism.' Led by Roy Cogdill, Yater Tant, and the Gospel Guardian, a substantial number of churches have come to oppose such cooperative programs of evangelism as the Herald of Truth and the homes for orphans and aged, as they are presently organized. During the past 15 years many debates have been held, churches have divided, and fellowship has been broken. This is the most serious division, numberswise, that churches of Christ have suffered. Whether the division is final, or whether it can be healed, is yet to be determined."[40]

Perhaps the note of hopeful optimism struck here was induced by the Arlington Meeting, conducted about the time Humble's book was being written, and in which he participated. Although one can applaud the good intentions and positive tone of that meeting (the book which came from it is one of the best tools for study of this controversy), time has revealed, however, that Arlington accomplished little in healing division, restoring fellowship, or reversing any of the trends which produced the division in the first place.

I enter this next section with trepidation, since what I propose to do is objectionable to some as an attempt to "number Israel" or "count the faithful" – thankless tasks which would perhaps be scripturally objectionable even if they were not impossible. Some even objected to gatherings such as the Nashville or Dallas Meetings (1988 & 1990) as attempts to "line up"

---

40 Humble, *Story of the Restoration*, p. 74. The note of cautious optimism struck here might have been due to the *Arlington Meeting*, held about the time Humble's book was written and in which he participated. However, the positive tone produced by Arlington was short-lived. An attempt at a follow-up meeting at Leakey, TX a year later produced the following exchange: "One preacher said, 'Give us the Scripture authorizing the things you are doing and advocating; that is all we ask.' A prominent preacher retorted, 'Give us Scripture! Give us Scripture! You can teach an old green parrot to say 'Give us Scripture.' That is all you fellows say. I was amazed! . . . Some churches could surely use an old green parrot to cry out, 'Give us Scripture! Give us Scripture!' . . . Few preachers are saying it" (Joe Fitch, "An Old Green Parrot," in *Plain Talk* [Oaks-West Church of Christ, Burnet, TX] 6:2 [April, 1969], p. 3; see Robert F. Turner, "That Leakey Meeting," *Plain Talk* 5:12 [February, 1969], p. 2).

churches and brethren into groups or to promote a "we-consciousness" which might be viewed as a precursor to behaving like a sect. I share some of these concerns, but in an attempt to provide some dimensions to the problem, I venture the following information.

Brother Mac Lynn began the task in the 1970's, since continued by others, of gathering factual data about numbers of congregations, etc. Using some of his information, I calculated that as of 1987 there were approximately 1,959 congregations which could reasonably be identified as opposing centralization and cooperative endeavors in the work of the church. Although the number of members in those churches was not easily available, I put pencil to paper and, based on older data Mac Lynn provided me several years ago, calculated that the average membership in a "non-mainstream" church was a fraction less than 95 members per congregation (and a fraction larger, in fact, than the average for "mainstream" churches – which simply shows that aside from the "100 Largest Churches of Christ" which used to be listed occasionally in the *Gospel Advocate* it is apparent that the average churches on each side are probably fairly similar to each other in size).[41]

---

41 The Guardian of Truth *Directory of Churches of Christ 1989* listed approximately 2,265 congregations in the United States; other information from Mac Lynn to Steve Wolfgang, September 29, 1987 (letter and enclosures: "Statistical Summary" and "Congregational Character" for 1987 edition of *Where the Saints Meet*); 1981 data reported in Flavil R. Yeakley, Jr., "Reasons for Optimism Regarding Prospects for Church Growth," *Gospel-Advocate* 123:11 (June 4, 1981), p. 327. The figures for average members per congregation are 94.97 for all "Churches of Christ" (12,706 congregations with 1,206,799 members), with the average for "mainstream" churches (10,165 congregations with 965,439 members) marginally smaller than those for "non-mainstream" churches (2,541 congregations with 241,330 members). Figures for 1997 indicate 13,364 total "Churches of Christ" with 1,275,533 members; noninstitutional churches number 1,959 (about 15 percent of the total congregations claiming to be "Churches of Christ." Non-class and one-cup churches comprised 1085 congregations. For a discussion of various aspects of "counting the Christians" see Mac Lynn, "The 100 Largest," *Gospel Advocate* 121:22 (May 31, 1979), 344345; Carl W. Wade, "Where Are We Now?" *Firm Foundation* 96:42 (October 16, 1979), p. 659; and periodic issues of Mac Lynn's *Missions Bulletin*, issued from 1977-1987 by White Station and Ross Road Churches, Memphis, TN.

Current calculations a quarter-century later would no doubt show some variances from these figures; however, they could not be obtained and calculated in time to be included

Among the members of these churches, there is enough interest in religious journalism to support a number of papers which still reflect the non-institutional viewpoint. At the dawn of the digitial age, the largest of these, issued monthly, were *Christianity* and *Searching the Scriptures* with about 6500 and 5500 subscribers, respectively. *Guardian of Truth* (result of the 1981 merger of the *Gospel Guardian* and *Truth Magazine*), was at that time issued twice monthly, reporting about 4500 subscribers. It has since reverted to its original name, *Truth Magazine*, and even in a digital age reports nearly 4000 subscribers, including several hundred who receive the magazine electronically. The Foundation which publishes it (the old "Cogdill Foundation") still publishes books, tracts, and Bible class literature, a new hymnal (*Psalms, Hymns, and Spiritual Songs*) and a nearly complete set of New Testament (as well as a projected Old Testament) commentary set; since 1986 the Foundation has operated the CEI bookstore in Athens, AL. The Foundation recently consolidated operations and sold its long-time location in Bowling Green, KY, to OneStone, Inc., which maintains a bookstore operation, as does Religious Supply Center in Louisville, KY. Some other journals, such as *Faith and Facts*, *Gospel Anchor*, *Sentry*, and *Torch*, previously published as monthly or quarterly print publications with smaller subscription lists, have transitioned to digital publication in a fast-moving digital age. Various individuals and groups also publish a variety of Bible class workbooks, tracts, hymnals, self-published books, and other Bible-related materials.

Florida College, in suburban Tampa, is an accredited four-year college which has existed for decades without soliciting or accepting contributions from churches It is patronized largely by members of churches of Christ which oppose such church support of institutions. Current enrollment is approximately 500 students from 35 states and several foreign countries.[42]

---

in this paper. Hopefully they will be available for discussion when this paper is presented.

42 In addition to those enrolled in the Biblical Studies program at Florida College, various congregations have provide opportunities for young men who wish to prepare to

A fairly popular feature in the training of younger preachers has been an "apprentice-type" relationship in which a congregation with an older preacher will employ a young man for a period of time (usually a year or so) to study with the older man, share preaching and teaching responsibilities, and "learn by doing." Several congregations, notably in Washington, California, Texas, Kentucky, Indiana, Florida, and elsewhere have had more extensive arrangements of "special classes" for the instruction and training of young men desiring to preach.

Although most churches of the non-institutional persuasion obviously do not participate in evangelistic projects such as Herald of Truth, various churches for years maintained wide-area radio broadcasts on clear-channel stations (Arch Street in Little Rock, for example). Over the last several decades, however, a more popular approach has been the proliferation of local "call-in" type programs on local radio (or, more recently, local cable TV outlets). Churches in several major metropolitan areas have found mass mailings of correspondence courses using city directories to "target" areas to be successful in reaching new converts. Much of this has been superseded in recent years by Internet-based studies or arrangements using Skype or other electronic/digital means of propagating the gospel.

In foreign evangelism, non-institutional churches have usually opted for other means than sending "American missionaries" overseas for extended periods (though non-institutional churches have supported about such men, and their families, in England, Ireland, Norway, Germany, Chile, Argentina, Australia, Japan, People's Republic of China, Zimbabwe, South Africa, and elsewhere). Sometimes foreign nationals have been brought to the U.S. for a period of study and then supported for a period of time in their native culture by American churches. Other native preachers converted (either by Americans or

---

preach. The congregation at Danville, KY, for example, offered special training classes, taught by the local preachers, elders, and other area preachers. More than 100 men have been in the program; many of them have preached, or are now preaching in fifteen states was well as Canada, Mexico, South America, Spain, and Germany.

foreign nationals trained in America) and working in their own culture are heavily supported by American churches. I would estimate that a fairly high percentage of non-institutional churches have supported men engaged in foreign evangelism.[43]

Obviously, churches of the non-institutional persuasion do not donate financially to benevolent institutions; instead, they have "practiced what they preached" and provided such care individually. In 1965, Eugene Britnell surveyed 60 preachers who opposed church support of institutional orphan homes and accumulated a list of 450 orphans and widows cared for by such Christians ("Our Defense to Those Who Falsely Accuse Us"). In documentation assembled for the **Willis-Inman Debate** (1966), Cecil Willis gathered information demonstrating that 17 children had been adopted or cared for by the faculty at Florida College, which at that time consisted of about 25 families; and that the eight families represented by the editorial staff of the **Gospel Guardian** had provided homes at one time or another for at least ten children who were not the natural offspring of those families. (This is perhaps also the place to notice that a reading of the **Gospel Advocate** and **Firm Foundation** for 1958-1962 demonstrates that the "institutional" brethren came very near fragmenting themselves over whether orphanages could be organized under a corporate board or must be overseen directly by elders of a church.) Currently, several individually-supported organizations such as "Sacred Selections," or "Help A Neighbor," and others, exist to enable individual Christians to cooperate in a number of benevolent enterprises and situations.

Current Perceptions

As I prepared for the Nashville Meeting in 1988, it occurred to me that some attempt to gauge how the non-institutional brethren saw their counterparts among the institutional churches might prove useful. To that end, I mailed more than

---

43 Information on various aspects of foreign evangelism by non-institutional churches was chronicled for several years by Sewell Hall in his monthly columns for *Christianity Magazine*. Other such information appears frequently in various other journals, both print and electronic.

100 questionnaires to various preachers, elders, and members of my acquaintance from coast to coast. As I explained earlier, I make no claim for it as a scientific polling device, but I received about 50 completed questionnaires from people in fifteen states, who took the time to share with me their perceptions of the past controversy, the current state of affairs, how they felt about the past, present and future of the churches embracing the two persuasions, and where they feel the "institutional" churches are headed. Even after a quarter-century, many of their comments remain informative and relevant, and I offer some of their comments here.[44]

As one might expect, they were not generally appreciative of institutional brethren, although when I asked them to list what they saw as positive features of institutional churches, most listed zeal, sincere willingness to reach the lost, and similar traits. Several of the preachers who personally participated in this controversy observed that (in the words of one who says he "was one of the first gospel preachers to be 'fired' because of my stand on the issues"), "we could have been more temperate and patient with those with whom we differed."

Most reported little, if any, contact with institutional brethren, although one older preacher in the West reported that "I have had a pleasant relationship with _____. We have coffee together and have discussed our differences. We have mutually shared problems which are experienced in both liberal and conservative camps. . . . I see no hope for [unity] if we mutually

---

44 In order to encourage the respondents to speak as candidly as possible, I promised that no one would be quoted by name. It is clear, however, that both my questions and many of my respondents' answers have been heavily influenced by the historical interpretation advanced by Ed Harrell, and extended by other historians, including myself. Anyone who really wants to understand the conservative mentality of non-institutional brethren needs to read, for example, "The Emergence of the Church of Christ Denomination" (reprinted many times as a tract; originally in *Gospel Guardian* 18:40, 41, 42 [February 16, 23 and March 2, 1967]; "Some Practical Observations on the Middle of the Road," *Gospel Guardian* 20 (September 5, 1968), 273-278; "Emergence of the Church of Christ Denomination Update," *Vanguard* 5:2 (January 25, 1979); and Harrell's 1981 Florida College lecture on B.C. Goodpasture, op. cit., as well as some of his observations contained in his biography of Homer Hailey, Churches of Christ in the 20th Century. Those not familiar with the brother Hailey's life and work might wish to consult the biographical entry in *ESCM*, pp. 378-379.

isolate ourselves from all communication." But a California preacher's comment is typical of several responses: "The more 'conservative-liberals' don't seem to be as susceptible to discussions. Still seem to have the attitude promoted by the Gospel Advocate of 'ignore them, don't acknowledge them, and they'll go away!'" Most of those who reported having discussions with institutional brethren found them amiable, despite the common notion that discussions promote disharmony. One well-known conservative preacher opined, "When we pull in our horns and show kindness and less disagreeableness, they generally are more receptive." But most seemed to be of the opinion that "bad attitudes" or "hot-headedness" were not major factors in the controversy, and certainly not the basic reasons which produced division.

Many respondents seemed frustrated that most institutional preachers did not, in their opinion, seem to realize what it is that disturbed the "conservatives." One young conservative preacher reported initiating informal discussions with an older "institutional" preacher who has had at least one formal debate on these issues. The older preacher admitted "not fully understanding" any distinction between the individual and the church, and reported "never getting bro. [Robert] Turner's point about the church not being composed of congregations" – both points which to conservative brethren seem basic and fundamental. But perhaps more than anything else, the respondents registered an air of resignation borne of their past experiences that nothing much has changed even in the best of circumstances; that institutional brethren seemed, in their experience, totally unwilling to yield in their allegience to their institutions. One Florida preacher, in a discussion with the superintendent of a church-supported orphanage, asked, "If all the money you are now receiving from churches could be replaced by money from individual contributions, would you take your hand out of the church treasuries and thus stop the division of churches over this matter? He answered no, he would not."

When asked where they see the institutional brethren heading, most responded by noting the growing fissures evident among brethren who have been united in the past in their support of institutions. Many agreed in essence with the analysis of one young preacher who left an institutional church after attending both Lipscomb and Harding Graduate School, and who from that perspective predicted, "they must divide – they are already divided in many cases. Their differences between one another are too great for them to continue to work together." One Texas preacher noted specifically that "the more liberal element in institutionalism continues to control highly visible institutions (colleges, etc.). The more conservative element in institutionalism is being left behind and is trying to form a coalition through lectureships and journals. Yet some of the most vocal conservatives are amazingly tolerant in having fellowship with the more liberal element."

Since I have already used this paper to act as historian, preacher, and reporter, I will go ahead and try my hand at prognostication! Many years ago, a well-known preacher from the institutional persuasion asked me two questions at the conclusion of a gentlemanly discussion of our differences: (1) Was this division preventable or inevitable, and what might have been done to preclude the division of churches? (2) Is it reversible – is there any possibility of the restoring of fellowship and a feeling of brotherhood and good will to any level even approaching that of a generation ago? I would like to answer the second question first.

My answer is, "No" – although I hasten to add that I would be happy to be proven wrong and to be relieved of my cynicism. A more experienced historian than I has stated the case fairly starkly, however, in terms with which I must concur. Remarking on the aftermath of the Arlington Meeting, Ed Harrell asked, "Does anyone seriously believe that ... the thousands of unscriptural promotions dreamed up will...suddenly, or slowly, begin to disappear? Of course not. No man could bring it off; not 20 or 50 or 200 men could bring it off. And not only could they not, they will not bring it about."[45]

---

45 Harrell, "Middle of the Road," p. 275. Even after heterodox theology among the Herald of Truth staff was publicly exposed by some of its staunchest former supporters,

Events of the intervening decades have borne out many predictions of separation and alienation among various persuasions in the "institutional" churches. Current circumstances are analogous in many ways to those that existed when H. Leo Boles addressed Christian Church preachers at the "National Unity Meeting" in Indianapolis in 1939,[46] three-quarters of a century ago, when he argued that the only way to unity was to give up the practices which divide us. Of course, "institutional brethren" do not react positively to such suggestions. Indeed, it was the recognition of the fact that this was not going to happen which caused thousands of conservative brethren to renounce the many loyalties in this world – to alma mater, congregations where they once worshiped, past friendships, even family – and go their own way, in the 1830's, the 1890's and the 1950's.

Such a movement to turn the clock back would require that institutional brethren in thousands of places make a conscious decision to place fellowship with their non-institutional brethren on a higher plane than the support of human institutions – and I know of no one, anywhere, who believes that is a realistic possibility. While I would be delighted to be proven wrong, everything except my occasional wishful thinking tells me otherwise.

Furthermore, the situation seems to be moving in the wrong direction for anything like this to happen. In the same manner

---

it quickly became clear that the critics were not about to abandon their allegiance to the principle of broadcast evangelism under a large, centralizing church; nor could any influential body of preachers muster enough influence to "kill" such a program. See *Memphis Meeting With Representatives of Herald of Truth: September 10, 1973* (n.p., n.d.).

46 H. Leo Boles, "The Way of Unity Between the 'Christian Church' and Churches of Christ" (Memphis, TN: Getwell Church of Christ, 1985). This pamphlet is a reprint of Boles' speech which was originally published serially in the *Gospel Advocate* 81 (May-June 1939 issues), and responded to in the *Christian Standard* 74 (May-June 1939). See also "Unity Urged for Church Branches" (*Indianapolis News*, May 3, 1939), and the *Indianapolis Star* 36 (May 3, 1939), p. 15; "Disciples Discuss Unity With Churches of Christ Leaders," *Christian Evangelist* 77 (May 11, 1939), pp. 499-500. For accounts of Boles' speech, see J.E. Choate, *I'll Stand on the Rock: A Biography of H. Leo Boles* (Nashville: Gospel Advocate Company, 1965), and *The Anchor That Holds* (op. cit.), 147-152.

that the "Joplin-style" meetings demonstrated considerable differences between "institutional" brethren and the "independent" Christian Churches (to say nothing of the "Disciples of Christ") – differences involving far more than just instrumental music – so most of us who have tried to follow what is developing among institutional brethren perceive an increasingly-accelerating shift away from New Testament practices and attitudes. As one of the respondents to my survey put it, "It isn't just supporting an orphanage anymore. The liberal church in town here split this congregation years ago over the orphanage issue – but ironically doesn't support one to this day! What they have done is to accept people we have withdrawn from, no questions asked; or accept in full fellowship people who have left here after hearing, preaching they didn't like on divorce and remarriage, the role of the Holy Spirit, examination of premillennial claims or of the Masonic Lodge – all of them 'shaken in' with the clear understanding that they will not hear any preaching on those or any other controversial issues. Don't let someone tell you it's just 'sending a few dollars a month to an orphanage' – it's how we look at the Bible, the church, living the Christian life, and much more. The longer it goes on, the more incompatible we will become."

That this is not just the isolated carping of a disgruntled "anti" was seen even in the 1986 "Expression of Concern" signed by hundreds of preachers of the institutional persuasion.[47] While their concerns are specifically directed toward the theistic evolution problem and other situations at ACU, they also state more general concerns:

"I. We are deeply disturbed over the liberalism that is so evident in the brotherhood today. By "liberalism" we mean especially the following items, though not excluding other

---

47 *An Expression of Concern* (Ft. Worth, TX: Gospel Preachers, 1986). See also Roy Deaver, "Two False Extremes: Anti-ism and Liberalism," *Spiritual Sword* 16:2 (January 1985), p. 6; Garland Elkins, "The New Anti-ism," *Spiritual Sword* 17:1 (October 1985), p. 17; Thomas B. Warren, "Anti-ism Shackles the Church; Liberalism Opens the 'Floodgates' of Apostasy," *Spiritual Sword* 17:3 (April, 1986), p. 1; Probably the most complete statement of the position of this "cluster" of brethren vis-a-vis institutionalism is Thomas B. Warren, *Lectures on Church Cooperation and Orphan Homes* (Jonesboro, AR: National Christian Press [reprint]; original edition, 1958).

specifics that could be mentioned:

A. "There is a drifting from the Bible-centered, definitive, distinctive doctrine that once characterized our preaching. Presently, uncertain sounds and weak messages emanate from many pulpits among us. Brethren are becoming accustomed to diluted and polluted preaching. We are rapidly approaching the point where many of our people, including preachers and elders, no longer know the difference between true Christianity and the corrupted forms of it so prevalent about us.

B. There is a concerted effort on the part of some of our brethren to restructure the organization, worship and work of the church along sectarian lines, thus tending to denominationalize the New Testament body of Christ.

C. A spirit of doctrinal compromise and fellowshipping of those in blatant religious error has permeated our ranks.

D. The world has made alarming inroads into the church. Instead of the church influencing the world for righteousness, as it should, the world has adversely affected many brethren in matters of morality and conduct of life.

E. The typical emphasis of the denominational world on recreation, entertainment, and solving the social ills of society has been incorporated into the thinking and programs of many congregations, supplanting the God-given work of meeting the desperate spiritual needs of those both within and without the body of Christ."

No "anti" could have stated the case better. Indeed, from attending lectureships and "Christian Scholars Conferences" over the years at Pepperdine, ACU, Lipscomb, Freed-Hardeman, as well as several regional "evangelism workshops," my observation is that these "concerned" brethren are exactly right in their analysis – particularly with regard to the "social gospel" aspects of institutional churches. Articles even in "mainstream" journals have encouraged, without rebuttal or rebuke from editors or anyone else, the use of church buildings not just for fellowship dinners justified as "love feasts" but for "Scouts, quilting groups, exercise meetings, senior citizens, family reunions, receptions, and youth basketball and volleyball teams" in addition to "seminars on aging, divorce recovery, self-esteem, personal finances, stress and biblical exposition of books" – as if all were Biblically justifiable.[48]

Furthermore, the trek deep into social activities has only accelerated and expanded, in many quarters, since I documented, 25 years ago, not-so-isolated incidents of secular adult education classes, English as a second language, and GED classes offered by the church; counseling centers, medical-dental clinics, daycare centers, and "counseling services" which provide, among other things, job placement services. Brethren who might have been scandalized earlier in the "NI" controversy by the use of the church building for a "Chris Christian Concert" or a "Day at the Movies" (both with an admission fee) or a youth rally featuring the "World's Largest Hot Dog" all in the name of the crucified Christ, passed those milestones some time ago.[49]

Nor is it simply that many institutional churches seem to be hip-deep in the social gospel. Some who seem unwilling to accept or even to wrestle with the implications of following "commands and examples" seem bent on short-circuiting the process by challenging the validity of such an approach altogether. An approach which gratuitously sweeps aside any attempt to discover the details of God's plan is ultimately as offensive to "conservatives" as some of our reactions may be to those who are set to "re-examine traditional Restoration

---

48 For example, Douglas F. Parsons, "Increasing Church Visibility," *Gospel Advocate* 130:3 (March, 1988), pp. 24-25. For an interesting and still-relevant exchange on "social-gospelism" among churches of Christ, see J.W. Roberts, "What is the Social Gospel?" *Gospel Advocate* 104 (July 2, 1959), 419-420; and Ed Harrell, "Thoughts on Dishonesty," *Gospel Guardian* 11:20 (September 24, 1959), pp. 312-314; and Harrell, "The Social Gospel," *Gospel Guardian* 12:15 (August 18, 1960), pp. 225ff.

49 *Ashwood Leaves* (Nashville, TN), February 2 & 9, 1986, and October 11, 1987; *Bering Today* (Houston, TX), July 1978; see Steve Wolfgang, "Social Christianity," *Weekly Reminder* 16:46 (August 16, 1978), pp. 1-3.

hermeneutics." Indeed, upon reading one such effort produced by an institutional brother on "establishing authority," one non-institutional preacher remarked, "I could come nearer enjoying unity and fellowship with a conservative Southern Baptist."

Furthermore, to the historian, the current trend toward abandoning any attempt to ascertain what is authorized by utilizing commands, examples, and conclusions drawn therefrom (dismissing them only to replace them with humanly-perceived "principles") is old news.

These hoary ideas, laden with nineteenth and twentieth century cultural values, are the very arguments promulgated a century ago by those who were moving to become what we know as the Christian Church (particularly the Disciples of Christ). Once any attempt at a literal understanding of the Bible was abandoned, these concepts were advanced to "defend" everything from instrumental music to women preachers to the "higher criticism" of the Bible. As merely one example, notice this excerpt from an 1893 *Christian Standard* article entitled "No Man Wishes Women to Keep Silence in the Churches," in which one writer argued, "A principle may set aside an apostolic precept. It may brush aside an apostolic decree. We do that constantly. We follow the apostolic example whenever we like it; when we do not, we depart from it."[50]

Given this historical perspective, it is difficult to understand how someone who argues that there is "no pattern" expressed in Scripture regarding the work of the church, and that we are therefore at liberty to do whatever seems best to us, can gainsay the identical argument, which is now being advanced by defenders of instrumental music in the worship[51] – or any

---

50 George T. Smith, "No Man Wishes Women to Keep Silence in the Churches," *Christian Standard* 29 (October 7, 1893), p. 798. David Edwin Harrell, Jr., documents numerous examples of such reasoning in *The Social Sources of Division in the Disciples of Christ, 1865-1900* (Atlanta: Publishing Systems, Inc., 1973), especially chapters 1 and 13 (Harrell notes in the Preface that "the first and last chapters, taken together, are an interpretive essay on the sociological development of the church").

51 For an instance of this argument, see Alan E. Highers, "The Status of the

other unauthorized practice, for that matter.

But the end is not yet: even more fundamental concepts such as the inerrancy of Scripture are being questioned by some. Although the inerrancy of Scripture and other related concepts have been challenged by some on the "fringes" of "Churches of Christ" it is still startling to read the following assertion by a professor in a "Christian college," and published in a journal long associated with that institution.[52] "It is consistent to believe that the Bible is authoritative in matters of faith and practice, but may be incorrect in geographical or historical details. Once a person abandons the concept of divine dictation, he must abandon the idea of inerrancy." This would not be the first instance of doubt being cast upon the veracity of Scripture by those who are freely accepted and granted the "right hand of fellowship" by institutional brethren. Nor is it a totally unexpected development among those who have been taught for years to believe it is a work of the church to financially support "the ministry of continuing study toward a doctorate."[53]

I believe these brethren who "Expressed their Concern" put their finger on an historical undercurrent which was also revealed in the aftermath of the instrumental music/missionary society division. Those who are on the "pro"

Instrumental Music Controversy," in Dub McClish, ed., *Studies in 1 and 2 Thessalonians and Philemon: The Seventh Annual Denton Lectures,* November 13-17, 1988 (Denton, TX: Valid Publications, 1988), pp. 480-493.

52 John T. Willis, review of William J. Abraham, *The Divine Inspiration of Scripture,* in *Restoration Quarterly* 29:3 (Third Quarter, 1987) p. 169. For previous discussion of similar statements, see the references to David H. Bobo's 1960 Abilene lecture in Banowsky, 109-110, 139-140, 145; and Warren Lewis, "Every Scripture Breathed of God is Profitable," *Mission* 5:7 January 1972), pp. 195ff; responses in March and April 1972 and rejoinder by Lewis in July 1972 issues of Mission; Lewis, "Let's Look at the Text - again!" *Mission* 8:3 (September 1974), pp. 86ff; R. Lanny Hunter, "Restoration Theology: A Schoolmaster," *Mission* 7:12 (June 1974), pp. 356ff.; editorially truncated response by Ron Halbrook and Steve Wolfgang, "The Approval of God," *Mission* 8:4 (October 1974), p. 123.

53 Bill Flatt, "Harding Graduate School of Religion Commencement, 1975," *Gospel Advocate* 117:26 (June 26, 1975), p. 404. On the preoccupation with academic degrees and "scholarship" among institutional preachers, see Ralph T. Henley, "Scholarship," *Spiritual Sword* 6:3 (April 1975), 35ff; and Henley, "How to Get A Cheap Degree Cheap," *Gospel Advocate* 119:18 (May 5,1977), 276-277.

side of both sets of issues soon discovered that they were not a homogeneous group, and found (or are finding) reasons to separate from each other. As was the case with men such as J.W. McGarvey or Isaac Errett, first generation leaders who serve as a "bridge" for a little, seemingly harmless, liberalism often discover that succeeding generations are not content to stop where their forebears drew arbitrary lines, and are determined to carry to logical extension the incipient practices of the former generation.[54]

Even before I mailed my survey forms for the Nashville Meeting, I received an unsolicited letter from a young, but influential, preacher in what I would identify as the *Firm Foundation/Spiritual Sword* "orbit." He was insistent to tell me what I already knew: "that a very deep schism exists now in the institutional churches of Christ and when the final division comes (and it will) it will be greater in scope than that which occurred in 1952-1954." This young preacher's observations on developments within the "left wing" of institutional churches of Christ simply confirm Ed Harrell's prediction more than 40 years ago that "the time will come when the editorial era of B.C. Goodpasture will evoke only embarrassed, apologies from sophisticated leaders in the Church of Christ."[55]

From a diametrically opposite perspective, a young man who left the "conservative" church in which he was raised , sojourned awhile among the institutional churches, and is now involved in a denominational group on the state university campus where he is a professor – came this analysis: that among institutional brethren there are "two factions (not counting the MISSION-types, who are mainstream to liberal evangelicals) – one set is as 'patternistic' as conservatives without the common set of 'examples, commands,' etc. The other is a 'grace-unity' type that wants to retain CofC identity/features without having to defend them rigorously. The latter is a Christian Church with acapella music."

---

54 See Ed Harrell, "The Middle of the Road," *op. cit.*, p. 274.

55 *ibid.*

Given these circumstances, asking about restoring fellowship with the "antis" is pointless. It would border on the absurd if it were not a logistical impossibility. And by answering the second question, we have come a long way toward the answer to the first. Was the division so totally doctrinal that it was caused by the sheer force of logic on the one side and stubborn stupidity in the rejection of that logic on the other? In truth, although logic and doctrine played an important role, division came not just because brethren disagreed (which they did) or because some people misbehaved (which also occurred). They divided because they had divergent concepts of God, the Bible, the church, how to live as a Christian, and a host of other things. That is the sort of thing that likely will not be reversed by this meeting or a dozen like it, unless I miss my guess.

So what then is the point of continuing this discussion, and what can we learn in meetings such as this? Perhaps nothing; or, possibly several useful lessons. (1) It might result in some people changing their minds, their lives, and their convictions about some of these issues – and not simply in one direction. (2) Perhaps more likely, it will simply reinforce convictions already long held. (3) It could provide an insight for learning about others believe, and why – which might be useful even if nothing else results. (4) From my perspective, it may help some who did not live through the past division (or have only childhood memories of it) resolve that it will not happen again in our lifetime, if we can help it at all. Perhaps such divisions are inevitable every two or three generations as time passes, new generations with different agendas and presuppositions arise, and greater levels of (perceived) sophistication are attained.

I would like to think that by learning from the past, by teaching "with great patience and instruction" (2 Tim. 4:2, NASB), and by recognizing the factors and circumstances which breed division, perhaps our children or their children can avoid a quick rush into another division which can never be healed. Perhaps the task is futile – some whose judgment I respect have said as much. But the attempt seems worthwhile still.

2

BIBLE AUTHORITY &
THE NEW HERMENEUTIC

DANIEL H. KING SR.

Introduction

For most of us preachers who dwell on the senior side of the
generational divide, it is shocking to hear the conversational
back and forth that nonchalantly takes place on various media
forums these days. Little did most of us know that modernity
would spell the relinquishment and repudiation of most
everything we have believed to be true and held to be sacred by
a certain element of the new generation of preachers.
Apparently one of two things has happened while we have been
busily engaged in evangelism, church building, and battling
back the trends of modernism and liberalism: Some of us have
neglected to educate, or else have failed in our efforts to
educate, the oncoming generation regarding who we are and
where we have come from, or else a frighteningly large element

of the new generation has simply rejected wholesale our identity as an undenominational, non-sectarian and biblically centered fellowship of Christians. Make no mistake about it: that is precisely what is at stake when the matter of scriptural authority, how it is established and applied, is up for grabs.

Looking about us, we rejoice to see a great number of young men who are steady at the helm, working diligently to convert souls to Christ and save some from the follies of denominational confusion (concentrating their efforts primarily outward), while a great many others enthusiastically view themselves as agents of change within the larger body politic (looking chiefly inward) who hope to salvage something out of the hopelessly ignorant masses of deluded disciples - hide-bound traditionalists who from rote memory cite the "five steps to salvation," the "five acceptable acts of public worship," and the "three legitimate means for establishing scriptural authority," etc., as if each of these points could be cited from the pages of a sectarian Confession of Faith or a Church of Christ Creed located in a vault somewhere in Nashville, TN, Athens, AL, or Temple Terrace, FL.

Important issues are in question here, and they *are* serious indeed, despite the light-hearted fashion in which they are being treated by some otherwise very bright and capable men. In fact, if one cannot express general truth taught in the Word of God in a profoundly simple way without being falsely accused of creed writing, then we are in deep trouble as a people. From our perspective, many have already reached the point where they are doing more than just "thinking out loud." They declare themselves daily and boldly in various social media and on blog posts in a way that indicates their convictions are at this point already set in stone. For them, there may be no going back. They have become so inherently cynical about anything they consider to be "church of Christ tradition" that they represent a genuine threat to sound doctrine (1 Tim. 1:10; 6:3; 2 Tim. 4:3; Titus 1:9; 2:1) among God's people both now and in the future. If you do not consider yourself to be one of those people, then by all means, be careful what you say in your "posts" on various forums and in your blogs: be sure that what you write represents your settled convictions on any given religious matter. If you are not, then you may well find yourself at some juncture spending the rest of your natural life defending what you carelessly and thoughtlessly have said. Eating your own bitter words does not make for tasty fare! Keep it to yourself if you are not sure of it. Better yet, ask someone with much knowledge and considerable experience to discuss it with you in a private setting; listen carefully and respectfully to their reply. You might discover some wisdom in what they say as they open their Bible and thoughtfully explicate what they have pored over perhaps hundreds of times before. It was not for no reason that Paul paired with Barnabas as he began his career in gospel work, or that Timothy and Titus at various times later paired with the seasoned soldier Paul in order to enjoy the benefit of his more extensive experience and knowledge.

It appears impossible for some among us today to comprehend the rather mundane notion that these simple formularies to which we have just alluded, and some consider mundane if not downright boring, might actually represent the distillation of truth as it is presented in a host of New Testament passages. All texts have been read carefully and studied with appropriate attention to detail by several generations of Bible students, and they have come to a general consensus on these matters and in consequence of this have preached and taught about them with absolute consistency with one another, never mind the distance from one another geographically and even culturally. There is, therefore, to their minds at least little else to say beyond this on these specific topics. Their simplicity is deceptive, however. We may have grown up with them and deem them so common as to be monotonous, but if you have seen the eyes of someone brought up in the darkness of sectarian error light up at their first hearing of these straightforwardly unpretentious formulae, and then see them surrender themselves in gospel obedience to the Christ whom they have always believed in but now know themselves to be fully obedient to -- then and only then will you be able to judge whether or not they yet have cogency for our time. Ask some of the Filipino brethren laboring tirelessly in regions like Luzon or Mindanao whether these simple truths have power to change lives and alter destinies still today; better yet, go spend a few weeks working beside them and see it with your own eyes. The fact that some of us seem to have "moved on" beyond these simple Bible narratives may be more of a testimony to the cynical nature of our present culture than a comment on the validity of the narratives themselves.

When we today merely state them as though they were an identifiable list located somewhere in the Bible in precisely this form, we may do some certifiable injustice to the larger truth they represent, but this is neither intentional nor malevolent. Moreover, to disregard them altogether because of their inherent simplicity or cast them in an unfavorable light merely because they are not found in a biblical list somewhere (exactly in this form) within the larger canon of biblical materials appears to us to be a clear case of spiritual negligence: nonfeasance, misfeasance, or malfeasance (pick your poison).

I was brought up in the country, and although I have been blessed to enjoy the benefit of life in the big city for the major part of my life, and a pretty good formal education, still I believe that my head has not grown too big for my hat yet. Others may disagree, of course, but that is their prerogative. The point is, I consider everyone my equal and try not to "talk down" to others, regardless of their level of education, sophistication, or training. I will press an argument to what I consider its limits, and in the course of the back and forth of a debate will attempt to crush the opposition's viewpoint since I consider it wrong, but not the person himself. That is the example that the Lord left us all in his aggressive assaults on the Pharisees and the Sadducees. He was always firm but never cruel. On the other hand, he warned against alluding to others with the insult, "Raca!" (A Syriac word, expressive of great contempt for another, comparable to our words, "stupid," "idiot," "brainless," or "moron," cf. Matt. 5:22).

Recently I had a discussion with a couple of younger (college aged) fellows with whom I disagreed on a certain issue. Immediately one of them shot back that I was obviously "ignorant." He later apologized (more or less) when another young fellow in the group told him who I was and explained that I had been to school. But that experience is rather typical in our time. Many younger men who have sat at the feet of liberal professors espousing various forms of philosophical existentialism, are unwilling to credit the older generation with very much in the way of "smarts." They are quick to label us as witless if we disagree. This has become the "new normal" in our coarsened culture. When I was young, I was taught by my parents to respect those who were older and more experienced. That was good advice then, and it is good advice now. And, by the way, it is taught in the Bible (Lev. 19:32; Job 32:4, 6; Isa. 3:5; Rom. 13:7; 1 Tim. 5:1; 1 Pet. 2:7).

I did not attend Florida College. I was raised among institutional Christians and attended institutional churches of Christ until I was 19 years old. Our family left the ranks of institutionalism precisely because of issues related to the liberalism that was sweeping through those churches at the time. (I would never have imagined then that they would have travelled as far as most of them have now gone, and I am greatly relieved that my family did not travel down that road with them). My first two years of college were spent studying Classical Greek, Biology and Anthropology at a state university. Since my lot had already been cast in the direction of David Lipscomb College, I studied among institutionally oriented preachers, and became the one and only "anti" preacher from the class of 1970 with a degree in Bible. I did not have the benefit of a season of working with an older preacher in my early years either. Like most others at the time, I was "on my own" more or less from the start.

Accordingly, as I began preaching work I developed a long list of "heroes" to look up to, men who had proven their worth to brethren over many years of dedicated service, untold hours of Bible study, much experience in preaching and teaching, and had lived lives of integrity and moral purity. Almost every one of those men has now passed over to the other side. I learned much from these great and good men, and their wise counsel kept me away from numerous potholes in preaching. Their "preacher stories" intrigued and delighted my young ears and their warnings at times made my blood run cold. Some young folks today have no older heroes that they could name. Their peers are their role models. Or, if they have them, most of us would view those fellows as loose cannons, perennial trouble makers, or purveyors of heresy (they are described in the Bible, by the way: 1 Cor. 11:19; Gal. 5:20; Titus 3:10; 2 Pet. 2:1; 2 John 7).

Consequently, they are like the foolish king Rehoboam who listened to the advice and counsel of his inexperienced peers (1 Kings 12), renounced the wisdom of the elders, and thus brought his kingdom to division and ruin. Pity the poor congregation that engages the services of such a man! Many of the well-worn stories from the Bible and even the popular fables from the ancient world teach us lessons about the danger of human hubris and the importance of humility. We would do well to learn from them. Augustine wrote: "Do you wish to rise? Begin by descending. You plan a tower that will pierce the clouds? Lay first the foundation of humility." These are wise words; heed them.

Why A New Hermeneutic?

Now more directly to the subject which I have been assigned. The discussion that follows is intentionally long in the written format. Since the intention was to publish these lectures, it is customary to be more comprehensive and wide-ranging in a written format than a single speech will allow. So, we have deliberately and by design attempted to cover every argument that we have heard set forth by those who have rejected the traditional method of determining authoritative belief and practice and opted for a new hermeneutical methodology. It is a bifurcated blend of, on the one hand what we consider to be a serious study of the "authority issue" as we will most likely be dealing with it in the years ahead, and on the other some words of advice to the younger men whose task it will be to fight this battle. Most of us who are speaking probably will have disappeared from the scene by the time these issues are hotly contested in the public arena. For now they are kept mostly in the realm of private opinion, conversations among friends and confidants, and sometimes strange sounding comments on Google Groups, Facebook, Twitter, and other such social media. Make no mistake about it: the evidence suggests that the battle has already been joined, but for now it is primarily a rearguard action rather than a frontal assault and it has not yet found its champion, its Goliath. So, it mostly lurks in the shadows for the time being.

It will eventually rear its head in anger, spoiling for a fight, but only when it has gathered sufficient force and numerical advantage to assure its safety; of that we may be sure. There are many examples of this tactical maneuver which could be cited from the past. Some forty years ago a book entitled, *Voices of Concern*, was published and distributed by Carl Ketcherside who at the time edited a magazine called *Mission Messenger* in St. Louis, MO. Ketcherside and his minions thought when they released the title that "the time was ripe," and although a firestorm started in its wake, they were right in their analysis. It contained 17 articles which proved to be little more than bitter tirades against the churches of Christ and the doctrines taught in them. In that book Charles Warren wrote that "...the object of the Church of Christ is all too often a God of legalism rather than a God of love..."[1] J. P. Sanders further charged that "The scriptures were...not written to be complete blue prints."[2] Also, "Legalism sees sin as a violation of the written code."[3] On and on the rants continued, filled with hatred and despite for all that we as a people had stood for throughout the years of the efforts expended to restore New Testament Christianity to its original purity. Some even went so far as to deny the verbal inspiration of Scripture. As kindred spirits, they one and all, insisted that we give up the silly notion of "restorationism" and fully embrace our denominational brethren in their present situation and cease trying to convert them to "the truth." At first this was viewed

---

1 Robert Meyers ed., *Voices of Concern* (St. Louis: Mission Messenger, 1966) 200.

2 Ibid., 39.

3 Ibid., 42

as a movement on the fringes, and clearly at the beginning it was just that. But over time these ideas captivated the rebellious imagination of that era, and this way of thinking through the decades moved from the ideological fringes to the center of institutional professor's and preacher's thinking and eventually has become "mainstream."

Just how influential this fringe element had become was not fully realized by most of our brethren until the Nashville Preachers Meeting (Dec. 1-3, 1988). Reuel Lemmons (editor of the *Firm Foundation*, 1955-1983), 76 years old at the time, gave everyone a shock. He called for a re-thinking of our position on Bible authority. He opined that the idea of authority being established by command, example, and necessary inference is an 18th century manmade rule. He stated in no uncertain terms that he rejected apostolic examples and necessary inferences as a means of establishing Bible authority. He related a discussion with a Christian Church preacher who challenged his thinking about necessary inference. Someone had stated that we learn that unleavened bread should be used on the Lord's table by necessary inference and asked, "Would it be scriptural to have ham and gravy on the Lord's supper?" The Christian Church preacher replied, "Why not? The Lord's supper was joined to a 'love' feast. " Lemmons cited this example in his denial that examples and necessary inferences are binding. At this point in his life Lemmons had given up so much ground already in his thinking that he was now willing to go all the way. He died on Jan. 25, 1989, less than two months after the meeting.[4]

At about the time of that gathering, two of the speakers in particular drew much attention to their heterodox views. The first was Randy Mayeux (preacher for the Preston Rd. church in Dallas). At the Meeting he said that "Command, example, necessary inference, and specific and generic authority is Greek to me." Mayeux, apparently emboldened to bare his whole soul, stunned many of his listeners at Lubbock Christian University

---

4 Mike Willis, "Personal Observations On The Nashville Meeting," *Truth Magazine* 33:2, pp. 34, 53-54)

on Oct. 19, 1989, when he alleged that although the churches of Christ claim that they have no creed but the Bible, they in fact do have one. He referred to a well-known tract, *Can We All Understand the Bible Alike?*, as an "ignorant" viewpoint, and charged that the Scriptures cannot be uniformly understood, which, of course, makes the apostolic charge that we "all speak the same thing" (1 Cor. 1:10, ASV) rather meaningless. Brother Mayeux equated the use of mechanical instruments of music in Christian worship with such expedients as the Sunday school and multiple communion cups. He suggested that the division which came about between the Christian Church and the churches of Christ in the late 1800's was principally economic, i.e., some churches could afford the instrument and others could not, hence, a spirit of rivalry developed. At the same time he affirmed that he publicly taught that baptism is for the remission of sins, but confessed that his heart "inclines otherwise."[5]

Bill Swetmon was another speaker who attracted much notoriety. He was so bold as to argue that the New Testament canon did not exist until the fourth century A.D. and so the New Testament documents could not have provided for the church through those earlier centuries any sort of "pattern" for our work and worship. Bill Long attempted to make the case that what God's people need to do is study the life of Jesus and do what you feel he would do (*a la*, "What would Jesus do?"), rather than worrying about the business of establishing scriptural authority before we act in spiritual matters. It became clear to all of us present at that meeting that a new day had dawned in the institutional churches of Christ, especially in the area of understanding how authority is established and how it is applied, and that the conservatives among them were being outnumbered and effectively overwhelmed by theological liberals and modernists.

Later still, as the question of women's role in the public worship of the church had become a hot topic of the day, Royce

---

5 cf. H. R. Osbourne, "The Continuing Apostasy of Liberalism," *Truth Magazine* 36:2, pp. 48-49; W. Jackson, *Christian Courier*, February 1990, 39

Money made the observation (that no doubt many were already thinking) with respect to this lively issue and its ramifications for the study of biblical commands and precedents:

> Is it coincidence that we have developed a controversy about the role of women in the assembly about the time we developed the idea of a new hermeneutic? It is certainly true that you can't biblically justify the leadership role of women in the assembly by using the old hermeneutic! If you cannot prove that it is right to do something with the old hermeneutic, you must adopt a new one, or abandon the idea.[6]

This is the direction that things have always tended to move in the past. Someone has observed that institutions are like an automobile that when it's tires go out of balance inevitably veers to the left, and never to the right. We may surmise that it is inevitable that this historical pattern will be followed among us in the years ahead, so we must prepare ourselves for it. Hopefully, what we shall present in the lines to follow will prove to be helpful to some as they press the fight for "the old paths where is the good way" (Jer. 6:16, ASV), as we pray for a godly and faithful remnant (2 Kings 19:30, 31; Isa. 10:20-22; 37:31, 32; Rom. 9:27; 11:5; etc.).

Jesus Legitimized the "Authority Question"

These days it is often considered to be an irritation of sorts for one to insert into our endless self-indulgent chatter the troublesome question of whether or not there is biblical authority for us to act in a given area of religious activity. When we raise that issue now we often are greeted with a blank stare that says to us, "What planet are you from?" The assumption that we need authority in order to act in the religious realm was, in fact, assumed on both sides of the issues in the original institutional controversies. When you read the written debates (something that I would highly recommend to everyone, preacher or no), they all begin with a short summary

---

6 *Christian Chronicle* (5/93)

of the principles of biblical authority, how it is established, and how it is applied. It made no difference whether one was in the affirmative or the negative. The actual differences between the two sides were in how it was applied in various instances, never in whether such principles existed at all, or whether they represented a set of humanly contrived analytical tools utterly alien to the Bible. Brethren generally agreed as to how authority was established from Scripture.

I could offer many examples to prove this, but in this place will quote just one. These are the words of brother Guy N. Woods, in the first speech of his affirmative given at Indianapolis, IN on January 3, 1956. He knew that in order for his words to carry any saliency for his audience, it was essential that he be able to give scriptural authority for his position. Had he said at the time, "I reject the notion that biblical authority is necessary for our actions in religion. I am asserting a 'new and different hermeneutic' in the present debate," his approach would have been rejected outright by everyone on all sides of the matter. Brother Woods would never have made any such assertion, though, because he did not believe that. He believed that authority was necessary, and that the principles of that authority were easily understood and stated. But he also believed that the Scriptures supplied justification for what was being practiced by those Orphanages that were soliciting and taking contributions from church treasuries that he was defending at the time. This is where he fell short of proof, but it was his affirmation nonetheless:

> I have a chart that I want to put on the screen here, chart number ten; and you will observe the principle. It is a familiar one, and hence there is no particular point in arguing this at length. You will note here the essential and the incidental. On the essential side, the command to go; but the manner of going is not indicated. We may walk, ride, or fly. We are commanded to teach. That is essential. The incidental: radio, classes, charts. We are commanded to baptize. We may baptize in a baptistery, a pool, or a creek. The Lord's Supper is given. The cups, the plates, the tables are incidentals.

The contribution is the essential. Whether we pass baskets or hats is incidental. We are commanded to sing, to make melody; and songbooks and parts are incidental. And the care of the needy is the obligation; and the type of home, the location, the size, the number of needy is not indicated. That is the principle, and that will be sufficient for the chart just at this particular time.[7]

It is clear from this and from a hundred other quotes that we could marshal to prove this point, that an amazing consistency of opinion existed as to the means whereby authority was established, even in the whirlwind of divisive controversy swirling around us then. The issues that were debated at the time had to do with when a particular example was binding, not whether examples were binding at all. They were about whether a pattern existed in the area of benevolence or evangelism and whether that pattern was being followed, not whether patterns existed in the New Testament. We debated whether New Testament churches helped non-Christians out of the treasury of the local congregation or as individuals, not whether it made any difference what the Bible said about that or any other subject. Whence came this general understanding that existed at the time of these great debates between the giants of that era? How did they come to have so much in common, while in more recent days we have almost nothing at all in common with so very many of our institutional brethren? The answer lies in the new hermeneutical principles by which so many of them now operate. They are far afield from this general consensus that once held sway in the churches of Christ and especially amongst the preachers who heralded the gospel in that bygone day. Unfortunately some of our own have begun to drink from the same poisonous wells and are showing identical symptoms of ideological toxicity.

Those who are pushing this new hermeneutic for our time argue that we were then weighed down by a crushing burden of

---

7 *Woods-Porter Debate on Orphan Homes and Homes for the Aged* (Nashville, TN: Gospel Advocate Company, 1956), 10-11.

legalism and traditional orthodoxy which has since been shaken off by a new, sophisticated, and more enlightened generation of preachers who care little for such things. They have transmogrified the entire process of biblical interpretation. Their whole perspective is delightfully different. They do not ask the "authority question" at all because they view the New Testament in a whole new light. They do not see it as a divine law to be studied and obeyed to the letter, but as a "love letter from God," or a pattern-less portrait of archaic religiosity, as a multifaceted mosaic of disparate religio-cultural anomalies, or some other such thing. Given this type of approach, it is not intended that we should care one whit about "every jot and tittle" as regards strict obedience or doctrinal soundness, but only concern ourselves with evidencing love and compassion, kindness and gentleness toward each other and our fellow men. Even historically significant doctrinal issues pale into insignificance in the wake of this new way of seeing religion.

This whole approach begs the question as to the derivation of this whole "authority question," however. A past generation of "church of Christers" did not raise this issue. The Lord dealt with it as if it represented an issue of genuine concern for those who had any real desire to please our heavenly Father. The occasion of this incident came near the conclusion of our Lord's public ministry. Here is the account as narrated by Matthew:

> And when he entered the temple, the chief priests and the elders of the people came up to him as he was teaching, and said, "*By what authority are you doing these things*, and *who gave you this authority?*" Jesus answered them, "I also will ask you one question, and if you tell me the answer, then *I also will tell you by what authority I do these things*. The baptism of John, from where did it come? From heaven or from man?" And they discussed it among themselves, saying, "If we say, 'From heaven,' he will say to us, 'Why then did you not believe him?' But if we say, 'From man,' we are afraid of the crowd, for they all hold that John was a prophet." So they answered Jesus, "We do not know." And he said to

them, "Neither will I tell you *by what authority* I do these things. (Matt. 21:23-27, ESV)

In his response to the Jewish leadership's query, the Lord switched topics on his inquisitors in order to throw them off their game, but dealt with the identical issue as he did so. They were asking if his teaching was from heaven or from men. What was the source of it? In his response, he asked them about the baptism of John, was it from heaven or from men. What was the source of it? In so saying, Jesus at once avoided the trickery of this band of quarrelsome detractors, and at the same time established forever the legitimacy of the major issue they had raised. Had God granted Jesus the authority to teach as he was doing? Was his message from God or man? Had he given to John the authority to baptize the people "for the remission of their sins" (Mark 1:4)? Was this practice from God or man? Both were perfectly legitimate questions. Jesus placed his own *imprimatur* on the distinction between what is authorized by heaven and that which is of human derivation, and therefore devoid of heavenly sanction. Authority for our beliefs and actions in religion must be established, like it or not. Jesus Christ himself recognized that fact. The issue cannot be shuffled out of the way by a simple wave of the hand. It is the Lord's question, not our own.

The Necessity of Logical Thought as It Applies To Authority

The human brain operates on the basis of interpretive rules. That is undeniable. This is the case in absolutely every instance of human endeavor. Our minds come to know things by various means, whether by what we read or what we experience. The two major problems of philosophical thinking, which philosophers have pondered for over twenty-five hundred years without solving them to the satisfaction of everyone, are the theory of reality and the theory of knowledge. Two simply stated questions are at the heart of the issues: 1) What is real? and, 2) How do we know what we know? This problem is, and always has been a major concern when we consider all of the various kinds of knowledge, but when we think about religious knowledge, we confront the additional problem of revelation from the supernatural world and from the mind of the all-powerful Person in that realm. The question is not whether such an Almighty One has the ability to convey his will to man, but rather is the question of how he may have chosen to do so. Did he decide to communicate through a logical message or body of teaching? Or, did he determine that it would be best to make his mind known to man through some subjective or even mystical manner of speaking? Another huge issue is whether such knowledge once conveyed through this medium is equally knowable by all men, or whether it is private to each individual and thus in a sense "different knowledge for different individuals"?

For most of our history as a human family, we have viewed such matters as purely rational and objective. But under the influence of a group of modern philosophers and theologians, the tide has turned away from a rational approach to Scripture in particular. As a consequence, a large body of the intelligentsia of our time has subscribed to one or the other of the forms of this subjective or irrational experience as the basic or main avenue of acquiring knowledge. For over a hundred years now, the influence of men like Jean-Paul Sartre, Fyodor Dostoyevsky, Albert Camus, Søren Kierkegaard, Friedrich Schleiermacher, Martin Heidegger, Rudolf Bultmann, Emil Brunner, Karl Barth and a host of others have placed emphasis upon subjective existential knowledge as determinative. Their influence has been amazingly effective in an otherwise "scientific age" where the scientific method and rational thought have been more generally celebrated. Numerous students of the Bible have been infected with their ideas, even though they may never have heard their names. Many evangelicals, on the other hand, in this area have placed emphasis on the Calvinistic notion of "authentication of the Spirit," i.e. that the mind of man is quickened or enlightened by the Holy Spirit as he reads a passage of Scripture, and thus comes to a conclusion regarding the truth taught therein. He has no ability at all to understand any spiritual truth until thus visited. Catholicism still teaches that a specially ordained interpreter (a priest) is essential for understanding, so that the individual is not capable on his own of embracing the fullness of divine truth.

The old rationalistic school of thought rejects all of this subjectivity, no matter how sophisticated it is made to sound, for at the end of the day it is unverifiable and cannot be tested by logic or scrutinized by reason. It holds that the Bible consists of propositional (possessing statements that affirm or deny something) truths which are equal in truth value to other types of propositions, such as those of the scientific variety. Historically, one group of scholars taking this approach considers the Bible to be a Book of wholly human origin, and therefore amenable to human error and subject to all sorts of contradictions and foibles. Some of it is valuable and some of it is worthless.

The other group under this rubric is the one that we have historically been identified with: those who see the Bible as propositional in its essence, and yet having been produced under divine guidance through the Holy Spirit's leading of the authors of the various books contained within it (2 Pet. 1:21). This does not, however, mean that we embrace rationalism as the means of ascertaining all knowledge, for if that were the case it would remove the divine element from the equation, but it does mean that we accept reason as an avenue or method of apprehending and comprehending knowledge as we glean it from the Scripture. Jesus said, "Ye shall know the truth, and the truth shall make you free" (John 8:32). There is an air of certainty and definiteness about that statement from the mouth of the Savior; it breathes out a sense of rationality and objectivity that is not found in these other approaches to knowing.

At the same time, there is a realization that comes from our study of the Bible that the reason we employ in our approach to Sacred Writ requires faith in order to function properly. After all, "Faith is the assurance of things hoped for, the conviction of things not seen" (Heb. 11:1, ESV). Reason, supported by the available evidence and empirical facts, can take us only so far, and then we must go on to our conclusion by means of faith.

The propositional statements found in the Bible must be accepted by faith. Many things found in the Bible are non-verifiable in the scientific sense. At the same time, the real power of the revelation is in its message, its truth content. "Faith comes by hearing and hearing by the Word of God" (Rom. 10:17). The nature of the Bible itself, the story of how it was produced, the fact of supernatural power being exercised in its production -- although all of these things are interesting and important in their own right -- must not distract us from *the message* wherein lies the power and the purpose of the revelation. The whole purpose of the Bible is to lead us to Jesus Christ, our Savior, our Lord, our Prophet, our Priest, and our King (1 Cor. 1:23, 30; 2:2; etc.).

But how do we finally arrive at this destination? What effectively takes us there? Testimony and faith are the channels through which these facts impress the heart and character of man. Testimony conveys them to the understanding, while faith brings them to the heart of the sinner, resulting in conversion and the creation of a new spiritual creature. All moral facts which form character and shape life are to be found in the testimony that constitutes God's revelation. But no fact can thus function, in the absence of its being testified to. "The love of God in the death of the Messiah never drew a tear of gratitude or joy from any eye, or excited a grateful emotion in any heart among the nations of our race to whom the testimony never came...No fact has ever influenced the heart of man or woman to whom it has not been testified...Testimony is, then, in regeneration, as necessary as the facts of which it speaks."[8]

Since such a large part of the Bible qualifies as testimony, in one way or another, it is all important in revelation. If there is no testimony there can be no faith, for faith is belief of the message as being true. Belief without testimony is as impossible as seeing without light. The strength, quality and power of a faith are in direct proportion to the facts and the

---

8 Alexander Campbell, *The Christian System* (Cincinatti: Bosworth, Chase & Hall, Publishers, 1871) 92.

testimony which produce it. If the testimony is valid and authoritative, the faith will be also. *True faith is the belief of true propositional statements, no more and no less.* The power of faith is not at all in the act of believing, but in what is believed: "How shall they believe in him of whom they have not heard?" (Rom. 10:14, KJV).

The difference between faith and knowledge is that in knowledge we ourselves are the witnesses to the facts, whereas in faith others are the witnesses to the facts and they report the facts to us in their testimony. We believe their testimony and have the feelings produced in our hearts by the faith, just the same as if we were the witnesses. But the testimony must be credible or confirmed before we can believe. *So, effectively, revelation is actually testimony, given in propositional statements, proposed to produce faith and obedience, leading to a changed life and a right relationship with God and Christ.*

On the still grander scale, common sense (the native capacity to reason things out to a proper conclusion) is the one essential that must be brought to the task of understanding the Bible. As Milton S. Terry wrote, "...all men are, and ever have been, in reality, good and true interpreters of each other's language. Has any part of our race, in full possession of the human faculties, ever failed to understand what others said to them, and to understand it truly, or to make themselves understood by others, when they have their communications kept within the circle of their own knowledge? Surely none. Interpretation, then, in its basic or fundamental principles, is a native art...a common art...a universal art."[9]

The Scriptures are expressed in the forms of ordinary human communication, with nouns, verbs, participles, purpose clauses and all of the other normal grammatical machinery that human language and general communication entails. Further, "We cannot believe that the sacred writers desired to be misunderstood. They did not write with a purpose to confuse

---

9 Milton S. Terry, *Biblical Hermeneutics: A Treatise on the Interpretation of the Old and New Testaments* (Grand Rapids: Zondervan, 1974), 174.

and mislead their readers. Nor is it reasonable to suppose that the Scripture, given by divine inspiration, is of the nature of a puzzle designed to exercise the ingenuity of critics. It was given to make men wise unto salvation, and in great part it is so direct and simple in its teachings that a little child can understand its meaning" (*Ibid.* 161).

To interpret the Bible correctly, we must therefore go at it in exactly the same way as we would in interpreting any other normal human communication. What this means is that we must employ the so-called "grammatico-historical interpretation" method in our study of God's Book. We study the grammar and vocabulary of the texts, and see them through the eyes of the historical period in which they were penned, and draw conclusions from all of the facts once they are properly assembled and analyzed. There is nothing at all mysterious about this methodology, and it is within the reach of the common man to be able to perform it. It amounts simply to logic being applied to written communication.

We perform these tasks daily without much deep thought being applied to them -- until some of us approach the Bible. They are native to us, almost at a primitive level. Let me illustrate. If I am out hunting, standing in a meadow and a grizzly bear is grazing at the other end of that expanse of green, then my eyes will automatically fix on him and his actions. I will analyze and interpret with great intensity what follows. His "body language" (a form of communication utilized by almost all of God's creatures) will tell me a great deal. He may be unaware of my presence. If that is the case, I will stand stock still until he moves along. I will not attract attention to myself. If he detects my presence, whether by his extraordinary sense of smell or sees my movements before I have seen him, then I will act quite differently. He may run away in fear. Bears are often afraid of human beings. I will not be foolish enough to chase after him. That might prove disastrous; after all, I might actually catch up with him, and I would not know what to do with him if I did catch him.

On the other hand, he may see me as a nifty lunch; bears are carnivores and have been known to take humans for food when they are especially hungry. If he makes a move in my direction, I will not flee from him, for that is the act of a prey animal. I know that I cannot outrun a bear. So, running away is pure folly. When I am in bear country hunting, I always carry a large caliber, high powered rifle along with a "bear caliber" sidearm. If there is sufficient distance for me to do so, I will raise my rifle at the first sign of a charge. If the distance is short, I will reach for my revolver and empty all six rounds into his upper torso. If that does not put him down, I will reach for my KABAR knife at my belt and attempt to go in close to him where he cannot simply "swat" me with his paws (called a "bear hug" and used successfully by some of the old "mountain men"). But I will know as I do so that he will most likely win the fight, and that I will either be killed or mauled horribly. That day will not end well for me!

What have we just done? We have created in our minds a possible scenario (hunters are confronted with this very situation all of the time) and suggested what we might do under each of those potential circumstances. We have read extensively on this subject. Our minds have interpreted the data and have made decisions in advance about what course of action to pursue given the various possibilities. You might react very differently than I would under similar circumstances: one gentleman said that he would shoot his brother-in-law in the knee and run. Somehow I think he was joking. But you get the point.

At any rate, each aspect of this situation had to be interpreted using logical, rational thinking, as well as testimony in the form of past experiences of others who have had bear encounters. Some faith had to be placed in the efficacy of that information. For example, an athletic human being runs at a speed of 12-15 mph over short distances, whereas a grizzly bear moves from a standing start at about 25-30 mph, covering exactly twice the distance in the same amount of time. The math is therefore undeniable. A bear will *always* catch us. So we must behave accordingly. How good are you at climbing a tree? It really does not matter: a bear is much better and faster at that also. You will lose that race too. So an intelligent human must behave accordingly. If you run away from him, a bear will act like a predator because you are behaving like prey. He will certainly chase you. An educated hunter will use rational thought, interpreting the data as he goes, and will probably live to see another day. Most do. One who does not educate himself to bear behavior, fails to read the signals from the bear when they are given, or does not carry with him the proper tools to deal with a bear encounter, will not make it out of the woods alive or will be severely injured. Such a person ought to stay out of the woods except when bears are in hibernation.

Everything we do as human beings, having been made in the image of a rational God, involves either inductive or deductive reasoning. Puerile sentimentality will not save us in the face of a charging grizzly! We may gush over how beautiful these creatures are, and foolishly opine that we are "in their forest as temporary visitors," or declare that "I would not ever hurt one of those majestic creatures" -- but a hungry apex predator will give us no compassion or mercy for the sake of our sweet sentiments. Only logical thought and swift action of the appropriate type will save us. Anything less than that falls short of a rational approach to the matter and may indeed prove disastrous or even fatal. This is simple, primitive, "educated common sense."

In the spiritual realm the same holds true. My fear of God is much greater than my fear of even the most ravenous of bears. That is the way it ought to be, according to our Master: "And be not afraid of them that kill the body, but are not able to kill the soul: but rather fear him who is able to destroy both soul and body in hell" (Matt. 10:28, ASV).

The ideas of "command, example, and necessary inference are inherent functions of our mental processes and have been since the beginning of the human race. Although not always under these particular terms, the concepts of "command, example, and necessary inference" are used in many fields of human endeavor today and have been so used for centuries. In law, for example, a lawyer or judge first asks whether there is a statement of law on the books that should be applied to a given case (command). Then he will ask, "Are there precedents from other cases that have been determined which should apply" (example)? Then he will ask, "Are there conclusions that may logically be drawn from the evidence that will apply to this case" (necessary inference)?

A doctor, likewise, will follow similar procedures. "Is there a general principle that governs a case such as I am now treating?" "Are there other instances of patients with similar circumstances which will provide me with guidance for this case?" "Are there logical conclusions I can draw from my experience that would help me in treating this patient?"

An architect will ask, "Are there principles or rules of construction that should guide me in the design of this building?" "Are there other buildings which provide comparable precedents that will help me in the design of this one?" "Are there conclusions I can reasonably draw to help in my design?" Again, this is simply "educated common sense" being put to the task.

Long ago the wise man declared: "The fear of the Lord is the beginning of wisdom; and the knowledge of the Holy One is understanding" (Prov. 9:10, KJV). Note the importance here of three things mentioned by the sagely author, aside from the requisite "fear of the Lord": (1) Wisdom; (2) Knowledge; and, (3) Understanding. All three of these terms define some aspect of logical thinking and the use of reason as a source of information about God and what makes him happy with us. The modern emphasis on emotions and personal subjectivism, and the consequent rejection of rational thought as a basis for believing in and serving God is utterly inconsistent with the biblical stress on its efficacy and saliency.

Silly sentimentality will not satisfy a hungry bear when it is charging toward a possible feast. The writer of Proverbs tells us that only rational thought put to good purpose will save us from the wrath of God. The mind of man must be supremely focused on what God has revealed of his mind in both the Old and New Testaments, that is to say, what will make him "delight" in us (1 Sam. 15:22; Prov. 11:20; 12:22; 15:8; Jer. 9:24).

Johannine Simplicity vs. Gnostic Inscrutability: A Lesson in Methods

I am constantly in awe of the Johannine materials as they deal with the complicated subjectivism of incipient Gnosticism (a complicated mixture of Hellenistic Judaism, Greco-Roman mystery religion, Zoroastrianism, and Neo-Platonism) as it manifested itself during John's final days on earth. The grand old Apostle does not delve into the intricacies of their strange and mysterious thought world, which is perplexing even to modern readers who try to follow the bewildering strata of their literature. Instead, he strings together simplistic sounding sentences that boil down to logical, almost syllogistic formulas, the major propositions of which no one could possibly doubt or dismiss without considerable assistance. Here are a few examples:

> That which was from the beginning, which we have heard, which we have seen with our eyes, which we looked upon and have touched with our hands, concerning the word of life--the life was made manifest, and we have seen it, and testify to it and proclaim to you the eternal life, which was with the Father and was made manifest to us--that which we have seen and heard we proclaim also to you, so that you too may have fellowship with us; and indeed our fellowship is with the Father and with his Son Jesus Christ. And we are writing these things so that our joy may be complete (1 John 1:1-4, ASV).

The conclusion we may draw from his simple language is that Jesus Christ, the Son of God, has been manifested in mortal flesh and "we have seen it" "with our eyes" and "touched with our hands" the one who is "the word of life." What we have here is a simple, yet thoroughly logical refutation of their theory that the Christ only dwelt for a time in Jesus of Nazareth, as a mere ghost is said to inhabit a haunted house. It involves

John's personal testimony regarding the physicality of Jesus' body. Again,

> And by this we know that we have come to know him, if we keep his commandments. Whoever says "I know him" but does not keep his commandments is a liar, and the truth is not in him, but whoever keeps his word, in him truly the love of God is perfected. By this we may know that we are in him (1 John 2:3-5, ESV).

Here, three separate logical deductions are drawn from the evidence as laid out in John's presentation. First, that knowledge of Christ is not speculative in nature, but practical and experiential. We come to know Jesus Christ as we observe his commandments. Second, one who claims to know the Lord through speculative knowledge of the Gnostic variety is a liar devoid of truth, because he either neglects to observe or intentionally refuses to comply with his "commandments." Third, one who professes to enjoy "the love of God perfected in him" is false to his allegation unless he "keeps his word," because it is by this means that "we may know that we are in him." Our relationship to him is made evident by our behavior, not only by our words. Assertions mean next to nothing unless they are supported by actions confirming their reality. Once more,

> Whoever says he is in the light and hates his brother is still in darkness. Whoever loves his brother abides in the light, and in him there is no cause for stumbling. But whoever hates his brother is in the darkness and walks in the darkness, and does not know where he is going, because the darkness has blinded his eyes (1 John 2:9-11, ESV).

Evidently the Gnostics claimed to "abide in the light" of God, yet they hated their brethren who stood with John on the issues of the day. They treated them shabbily and gave no evidence of having any love at all for them. John declares that such folk have revealed their true colors for all to see. Brotherly love, or lack thereof, is evidence of genuine religion, whether it is there or not. Therefore, "whoever says he is in the light and hates his brother is still in darkness." Their high sounding declarations about divine "light," special "knowledge," and intimate "inside information" about the deity are all valueless in the face of the simple syllogism that "God is light and in him is no darkness at all" (1 John 1:5). God is not to be found in the darkness of hatred, but in the light of love.

John rebuffed the subjectivism that reared its ugly head in his day and we ought to learn to do the same. Truth is propositional, coherent, logical, rational, syllogistic, and reasonable. It was then and it is now. If a truth cannot be boiled down to simple and understandable language that is almost formulary in nature (e.g., hear, believe, repent, confess, be baptized), as John was able to do throughout his literary endeavors, then we ought to wonder whether it is the truth or not. If, on the other hand, it can be thus simplified, then we ought not to laughingly cast aspersions against it, as though it represented nothing more than a creedal statement. Rather, we ought to use that very simplicity as did John to argue for its validity based on its biblical rationale. Paul seems to be using a simplistic formula to describe some important aspects of the life of Christ in 1 Timothy 3:16 (ESV):

> Great indeed, we confess, is the mystery of godliness:
>
> He (or "God") was manifested in the flesh,
>
> vindicated by the Spirit,
>
> seen by angels,
>
> proclaimed among the nations,
>
> believed on in the world,
>
> taken up in glory.

I suppose that if Paul could utilize this unpretentious method in his teaching (some have thought that he did so as a memory aid, others have speculated that he is quoting from a popular hymn among early disciples of Christ), without being unfairly described as a "creedalist," then we might deign to do so also.

Simple formulas are not something that we ought to be embarrassed about. Simplification is the key to understanding deeper truths.

The Jewish Heritage: Principles of Interpretation and Application of Scripture

The existence of what might be called "rules of interpretation and application" are neither new nor revolutionary in the Restoration Movement. We did not invent the concept nor were we the first to approach the subject systematically. Jewish rabbis early on developed a number of rules to help them as they interpreted the Hebrew Bible, and most of those are still honored as sound principles of literary interpretation even into our own time. The Classical state of the Hebrew language was verb oriented in its essence. Verbs mostly describe various types of action (or states of being). That meant that the rabbinical approach to interpretation also stressed action in the sense of application of the word spoken or written rather than enumerating and elucidating complicated systems of beliefs. Truth may be an idea, but it is not in this sense that the Hebrew mind primarily considered it. Truth was seen as an experience, and best conveyed through a presentation of history rather than through discussions of profound concepts. The Germans have an excellent word for it: *Heilsgeschichte*, or "sacred history." To the Hebrew thinker, a relationship with God, especially as it is defined in historical terms, was far more important than philosophical or even theological notions. Telling and retelling the stories of Abraham, Isaac, Jacob, Joseph, and the other heroes of the Hebrew Bible, as well as learning the lessons of the two competing Israelite kingdoms was central to Hebrew theology. We learn about God in the Old Testament, not through theological generalities, but by re-living the relationship he had with his ancient people throughout their long history together.

The New Testament, on the other hand, was written in Greek and from a Western standpoint. All of this Hebrew way of thinking and expressing oneself sounds very strange to us when we first hear of it, because it is so opposite to our own thoroughly Hellenized way of thinking. We moderns think like Greek philosophers on account of the thoroughgoing victory of Western thinking over that of Eastern or Semitic thinking. If we have been brought up hearing the stories from the Old Testament, then we have grown comfortable with it, even though it may be otherwise alien to our thought processes.

During the rabbinic era both language and culture had changed greatly from the days of Moses and the prophets. Both Greek and Latin were in currency, even though they spoke in Aramaic principally. Hellenism had changed the cultural milieu surrounding the Jewish people, and the Roman influence was becoming predominant, even though Greek was still the major language of commerce and some form of *koine* was the spoken dialect of the street and of everyday life in a pervasively Greco-Roman world. This being true, understanding the old Hebraic notions found in the Hebrew Bible had become continuously more challenging, even for those immersed in the literature of that earlier era. There was also the issue of real-life application of texts to various circumstances in a dramatically different set of cultural and conceptual circumstances.

In the world of the Old Testament the Jewish people lived under Hebrew rulers for most of their history. The law of the Lord was at first the law of the land in the new settled country of Canaan. In Exile, however, all of that changed rather radically. The law became a religious discipline practiced only by pious Jews. During that period they had gone from Assyrian to Babylonian to Median and then to Persian overlords. After a large number returned to their homeland, albeit under foreign sovereignty, they bore up under Greek hegemony, and then the back and forth of lordship under Ptolemaic Egyptians and Seleucid Syrians until 63 B.C., when the Romans claimed the land of Palestine for themselves. All throughout this confusing period people were studying the Bible, but many were greatly challenged by all of the change that had occurred since the writings were originally penned.

Rabbi Hillel the Elder (ca. 110 B.C.-10 A.D.), founded a

pharisaical school of biblical interpretation named after him, which was generally opposed by a much more austere school of thought founded by the sagely Shammai (ca. 50 B.C.-30 A.D.) and his disciples. Rabbis of the Babylonian Talmud set the work of Hillel on a par with that of the princely biblical figure Ezra the Scribe. The two schools were reflective of the nature of their founders: "Let a man be always humble and patient like Hillel, and not passionate like Shammai."[10] Hillel's gentleness and patience are illustrated in the ancient story of two men who wagered on whether Hillel could be made to lose his temper. Though they questioned him incessantly and made insulting allusions to his Babylonian origin (he lived in Jerusalem at the time), they were not able to unsettle him in any way or cause him to become angry. Hillel's philosophy was to "love peace, seek peace, love mankind and thus lead them to the law." He was named *nasi* ("prince" or "president") of the Sanhedrin in 30 B.C. and held that office until his death. Unfortunately his philosophy did not win the day. At his death in 10 A.D. the Shammaites took control of the Sanhedrin council and remained in power until the fall of Jerusalem and the destruction of the Temple in 70 A.D. Later rabbis honored him and blistered the house of Shammai for its unyielding ways: "He who observes the teaching of the house of Shammai, themselves deserve death."[11] The approach of Hillel to the Hebrew Bible was adopted in the academies at Yavneh and in Galilee during the second and third centuries. Therefore, it was the Hillel-type Pharisaism that became the "Judaism" of subsequent generations.

Gamaliel the Elder (also bore the titles of *Nasi* and *Rabban*) was his successor as leader of his rabbinic school of thought and application. He was the teacher of the Apostle Paul in his youth (Acts 5:34-40; 22:3). He was also regarded highly in the tradition: "Since Rabban Gamaliel the Elder died, there has been no more reverence for the law, and purity and piety died

---

10 *Shabbat* 30b; *Aboth de Rabbi Nathan* 15.

11 *Jerusalem Talmud, Berekhot* 1:4

out at the same time."[12] There is a reference in the traditional materials that Gamaliel taught a student who displayed the sort of "impudence in learning" that may have characterized the impassioned Saul,[13] who went against all that the gentle house of Hillel and Gamaliel stood for when he led the charge against what he considered to be the Christian heresy. Whether this referred to Saul or not cannot be determined with certainty.

Rabbi Hillel laid out Seven Rules for the correct interpretation of Scripture. This is the "simple" *(peshat)* level of understanding, reflected in the *Mishna.* The first rule, *kal v'chomer* is the only rule that can be derived purely on the basis of *severa,* or logical inference, while all of the other *middot* ("norms") require a tradition handed down from one's teacher. In Romans and Galatians especially, the apostle Paul makes use of many of the rabbinical exegetical methods, interpretive techniques, and arguments based upon tannaitic conceptions, with the express intention of impressing his readership with his own competence and authority in this realm of juridical reasoning and biblical interpretation.[14]

Rabbi Ishmael, expanding on Hillel's work, compiled Thirteen Rules for the elucidation of the Torah and for making *halachic* deductions from it. This is the "hinted" or "allegorical" *(remetz)* level of understanding, reflected in the *gemara.* Later still, Rabbi Eliezer ben Jose Ha-Gelili set forth Thirty-two Rules for *haggadic* ("reflective") exegesis, many of them being applied also to *halakic* ("practical") interpretation as well. This is the "parabolic" level of biblical understanding, demonstrated in the *midrash.* Many of these rules of interpretation are given different titles (such as *Kal va-chomer meforash,* "argumentum a minori ad majus," *Gezerah shawah* "argument from analogy," etc.) commonly accepted in biblical interpretation. The sages of

---

12 *Sotah* 15:18

13 *Shabbat* 30b

14 cf. D. H. King, "Paul and the Tannaim: A study in Galatians," *WTJ* 45 (1983), 340-70.

the Zohar went even further, enumerating Forty-two Zohar Laws for gaining the mystical or secret *(sodh)* understanding of the text. This final step has little to commend it. It launches the reader into the area of rife speculation, and in our estimation, offers little worthwhile understanding of the text itself.

The rules laid out by these rabbinic thinkers were formulated under the influence of Greek methods of reasoning being applied to various writings and their consequent influence in the prevailing societies in which they lived and worked. A Greek word, *epistemē*, meaning "knowledge or understanding" combined with the term *logos* (signifying a "study or discourse") give us our technical English word *epistemology*, referring to a study of knowledge and of the various theories of how knowledge comes into the mind of man. The philosophically oriented Greeks were central in the exploration of the issues involved in this process. The dialogues of Plato (ca. 424-348 B.C.), for example, represented informal examples of the discipline, whereas the works of the philosopher Aristotle (384-322 B.C.) contain the earliest known formal studies of logic and its rules. All of modern formal investigations into logical thinking follow and expand on the original work isolated and enunciated in this branch of learning by Aristotle. Logic (from the Greek word *logikē*) refers to the study of the various modes of reasoning, and is often divided into three parts: induction, abduction, and deduction.

Deductive reasoning concerns itself with what follows necessarily from given premises (if a, then b), and is in some sense the direct application of knowledge in the production of new knowledge. "If-then" deductive reasoning is how scientists can test alternative hypotheses. Inductive reasoning, on the other hand, involves trying to create general principles by starting with many specific instances. Induction is usually described as moving from the specific to the general, while deduction begins with the general and ends with the specific, i.e., arguments based on experience or observation are best expressed inductively, while arguments based on laws, rules, or other widely accepted principles are best expressed deductively. Abduction is a form of logical inference that goes from a description of raw data to a hypothesis that *seems* to account for the data. Abduction provides an argument whose premises give only some degree of probability, but not certainty, to its conclusion. Abductive reasoning, therefore, has no application to our present study, since what is only theoretical cannot be bound as a divine requirement.

Deduction and induction, however, are the basis for all of the modern systematic studies of the various rules and principles of interpretation which may be applied to Sacred Scripture. Scripture itself does not formally define, list or outline these rules or principles. Although, it does offer many examples of them being put to use by the authors of the biblical literature. The Bible is, after all, in one sense no more than a body of written communications, and since this is true, the general rules for interpreting and understanding literary works would apply equally to this corpus of materials as to any other. Most of these rules are simple and yet profoundly helpful. A few illustrations from one of the popular manuals of this discipline will suffice for our purposes here:

Under Lockhart's Rules:

Rule 8: Let an author's own explanation of his meaning take precedence over any other interpretation.

Rule 9: The interpretation of a passage must accord with the writer's purpose.

Rule 10: The simplest and most natural interpretation of a passage must be preferred.

Rule 11: Interpret so as to make the sense clear.

Rule 12: Any interpretation must be in harmony with grammar, rhetoric, logic and consistency, if the nature of the case permit.

Rule 13: An interpretation should conform to known laws, customs, opinions, history, country, biology, circumstances and character of the author at the time.

Rule 14: An interpretation must not be influenced by a preconceived opinion.

Not one of us would argue with any one of these "rules." It is clear from this that these "rules" are merely common sense conventions characteristically employed in dealing with written materials. Our tendency to want to isolate, analyze and generalize about such things is a carryover from the Hellenistic way of thinking which prevailed in the New Testament era, especially in terms of inductive reasoning. Many more of these principles have been isolated and described by various authors in their analytical studies of the Bible literature. When you boil common sense down to a simple list, then you have the gist of this brand of thinking and its *modus operandi*.

The following works are helpful in this regard. Most of them utilize different ways of saying the same things in slightly different ways and delineating the identical rules. A comprehensive bibliography of works of this type would fill many pages:

Berkof, Louis. *Principles of Biblical Interpretation*. Grand Rapids: Baker, 1950.

Hartill, J. E. *Principles of Biblical Hermeneutics*. Grand Rapids: Zondervan, 1960.

Farrar, F. W. *History of Interpretation*. Grand Rapids: Baker, 1885 (reprinted 1961).

Kaiser, Walter C., and Moises Silva. *An Introduction to Biblical Hermeneutics: The Search for Meaning*. Revised edition. Grand Rapids: Zondervan, 2007.

Klein, W. W., Blomberg, C. L., Hubbard, Jr., R. L. *Introduction to Biblical Interpretation*. Revised edition. Nashville: Thomas Nelson, 2004.

Lockhart, Clinton. *Principles of Interpretation: As Recognized Generally by Biblical Scholars, Treated as a Science, Derived Inductively from an Exegesis of Many Passages of Scripture*. 2nd edition. Delight, AR: Gospel Light Pub. Co.,

1915.

Longenecker, Richard N. *Biblical Exegesis in the Apostolic Period.* Grand Rapids: Eerdmans, 1975.

Ramm, Bernhard. *Protestant Biblical Interpretation: A Textbook of Hermeneutics.* 3rd edition. Grand Rapids: Baker, 1970.

Stein, Robert H. *A Basic Guide to Interpreting the Bible.* Grand Rapids: Baker, 1994.

Terry, M. S. *Biblical Hermeneutics.* Grand Rapids: Zondervan, 1883 (reprinted 1974).

Virkler, H. A., Ayayo, K. Gerber. *Hermeneutics: Principles and Processes of Biblical Interpretation.* 2nd edition. Grand Rapids: Baker, 2007.

Wood, A. Skevington. *The Principles of Biblical Interpretation as Enunciated by Irenaeus, Origin, Augustine, Luther and Calvin.* Grand Rapids: Zondervan, 1967.

Implication and Silence in Scripture

One of the controversies that has raged in the world of "Christendom" for centuries is the matter of whether or not the "silence" of the Scriptures must be respected or ignored. Some allege that whatever is not expressly *forbidden* is allowed in religious practice; others contend that anything not *authorized* is not permitted. The first approach is very "liberal" in its dimensions: it permits a whole range of options. The second approach is more stringent and limiting; for this reason one would not expect it to be very popular (and it has not been!). The dispute over which approach was to prevail in Christian thinking surfaced early in the post-apostolic age. Tertullian (ca. A.D. 150-222) spoke of those who contended that "the thing which is not forbidden is freely permitted." He replied: "I should rather say that what has not been freely allowed is forbidden."[15] Here is the quotation in full:

> This treatise, therefore, will not be for those who are not
> in a proper condition for inquiry, but for those who, with
> the real desire of getting instruction, bring forward, not
> a question for debate, but a request for advice. For it is
> from this desire that a true inquiry always proceeds;
> and I praise the faith which has believed in the duty of
> complying with the rule, before it has learned the
> reason of it. An easy thing it is at once to demand where
> it is written that we should not be crowned. But is it
> written that we should be crowned? Indeed, in urgently
> demanding the warrant of Scripture in a different side
> from their own, men prejudge that the support of
> Scripture ought no less to appear on their part. For if it
> shall be said that it is lawful to be crowned on this
> ground, that Scripture does not forbid it, it will as
> validly be retorted that just on this ground is the crown
> **unlawful, because the Scripture does not enjoin it.**
> What shall discipline do? Shall it accept both things, as
> if neither were forbidden? Or shall it refuse both, as if
> neither were enjoined? But "the thing which is not
> forbidden is freely permitted." **I should rather say
> that what has not been freely allowed is
> forbidden.**

It is clear from this that Tertullian was battling against an
encroaching sentiment that was much more liberal than his
own, that he was intent upon maintaining what he considered
to be a Scriptural mindset on the subject, and that he averred
that a biblical approach required that "what has not been freely
allowed is forbidden," that is to say, divine silence is prohibitive
rather than permissive.

During the early Reformation period, Martin Luther (1483-
1546) taught that "whatever is without the word of God is, by
that very fact, against God." He frequently appealed to
Deuteronomy 4:2 (KJV): "Ye shall not add unto the word which

---

15 Tertullian, *The Chaplet* 2

I command you, neither shall ye diminish aught from it." But the grand reformer gradually modified his view. Luther was wedded to many ancient church traditions and practices that had characterized Catholicism. Among them was infant baptism, which of course he could find no authority for at all in the Scriptures. They were as silent as a tomb about the practice, just as they were about many other things that persist until this day in the Lutheran church.

At a later time Luther tentatively wrote: "Nothing ought to be set up without scriptural authority, or *if it is* set up, it ought to be esteemed free and not necessary" (emphasis added). Finally, when had given due consideration to the implications of what he had earlier repeatedly and rightly said, he declared sheepishly: "What is not against Scripture is for Scripture, and Scripture for it."[16] How tragic it is that Luther's thinking evolved so much over his lifetime and that the eventual course of doctrinal digression that he espoused near the end is now being actively pursued by so many today! Great men do indeed often have "feet of clay."

Ulrich Zwingli (1484-1531) of Switzerland felt that practices "not enjoined or taught in the New Testament should be unconditionally rejected." Yet not even he grasped the full implication of this maxim, for he sanctioned infant baptism— which is neither enjoined nor taught in the New Testament. Yet this is not surprising. When a divine principle runs up against the stone wall of a favored religious practice or doctrinal position, very often the Word of God is worsted by the experience. At the same time it must be remembered that God will have the ultimate and definitive say in the matter.

In the final analysis, the issue is not what different famous men have had to say about this issue, but: does the Bible itself sanction the principle that the silence of the Scriptures is prohibitive? That is what counts. And on this matter the Bible is not silent:

---

16 A. H. Newman, *A Manual of Church History,* vol. 2 (Philadelphia: American Baptist Publication Society, 1902), 308.

A. "I commanded not."

Jeremiah was among the prophets who condemned the common ancient Near Eastern practice of sacrificing of children in worship; he protested: "And they have built the high places of Topheth, which is in the valley of the son of Hinnom, to burn their sons and their daughters in the fire; which I commanded not, neither came it into my mind" (Jer. 7:31, ASV). A screaming baby being burnt alive was thought to be the most significant offering to some of the gods of Canaan. In this context, it is clear that the words "commanded not" are precisely equivalent to a direct negation: silence was intended to be understood here as strictly prohibitive. Human children were not to be offered as sacrifices to God. This act was an abomination to the Lord (Lev. 18:21; Deut. 12:31; Jer. 32:35; Ezek. 23:39; etc.), whether it was done in honor of another deity or to himself.

The context of Jeremiah 7:31, of course, has to do with paganism; but that would not matter. Offering children as sacrifices to Jehovah God was prohibited by his silence regarding it. The book of Leviticus outlines the host of acceptable sacrifices: human sacrifice is never mentioned, other than as being a disreputable practice.

In this instance the text speaks with absolute clarity: silence prohibits.

B. "The Lord set aside the tribe of Levi, to bear the ark of the covenant."

First Chronicles 15 contains an interesting comment on an incident that occurred during the administration of king David at the time that he was reaching the height of his power and was therefore especially subject to the sin of pride. It has to do with the introduction of the sacred Ark of the Covenant into the city of Jerusalem, thus centralizing Israel's religion in the king's new capital. The record has its background in 2 Samuel 6. David was transporting the ark from the little hamlet of Kirjath-jearim ("city of forests") to Jerusalem (vv. 1-5).

The means of conveyance chosen by King David was on a cart, which, of course, was in violation of divine authority. The law had authorized the transportation of the Ark only on the shoulders of the priests, by means of rods which passed through rings on the side of the chest (Exodus 25:12-14). All other means were prohibited by divine silence.

Uzzah, who apparently was driving the oxen, touched the Ark to steady it when the beasts stumbled. Immediately he was struck dead by the Lord, a divine decision which did not please David at first (2 Sam. 6:6-8). The king must have felt some guilt after further consideration, though, since he had been the one who had initiated this new mode of transportation. Later, however, David frankly acknowledged that he had gone wrong since he had not sought the Lord according to the divine ordinance:

> Then David summoned the priests Zadok and Abiathar, and the Levites Uriel, Asaiah, Joel, Shemaiah, Eliel, and Amminadab, and said to them, "You are the heads of the fathers' houses of the Levites. Consecrate yourselves, you and your brothers, so that you may bring up the ark of the LORD, the God of Israel, to the place that I have prepared for it. **Because you did not carry it the first time, the LORD our God broke out against us, because we did not seek him according to the rule.**" (1 Chron. 15:11-13, ESV)

What was "the rule"? According to the law of Moses, "The Lord set aside the tribe of Levi, to bear the ark of the covenant" (Deut. 10:8). Only the Levites among the 12 tribes were authorized to carry the Ark. It is true that there is no passage that specifically forbade the other tribes to transport the sacred chest. David said: "None ought to carry the ark of God **but the Levites**, for them has the Lord chosen to carry the ark. . ." In the light of David's statement, the silence of Deuteronomy 10:8 was clearly prohibitive.

C. "Said nothing about priests."

The writer of the Epistle to the Hebrews argues that the

Levitical Priesthood and the Law of Moses were so intertwined that for one to be changed the other would necessarily have to change with it. He points out that the Law had to be changed because Jesus Christ arose from the tribe of Judah, a tribe which Moses was silent about concerning the priesthood and all of its attendant duties:

> For when there is a change in the priesthood, there is necessarily a change in the law as well. For the one of whom these things are spoken belonged to another tribe, from which no one has ever served at the altar. For it is evident that our Lord was descended from Judah, **and in connection with that tribe Moses said nothing about priests**. This becomes even more evident when another priest arises in the likeness of Melchizedek, who has become a priest, not on the basis of a legal requirement concerning bodily descent, but by the power of an indestructible life. For it is witnessed of him, "You are a priest forever, after the order of Melchizedek." For on the one hand, a former commandment is set aside because of its weakness and uselessness (for the law made nothing perfect); but on the other hand, a better hope is introduced, through which we draw near to God. (Heb. 7:12-19, ESV)

This raises the important question of the explicit and implicit teaching of Scripture. So, let us take a moment to explore it:

1) The Bible teaches both explicitly and implicitly.

Some subjects in the literature of the Bible are taught directly or explicitly. For example, the apostles were explicitly taught, that is to say by command, to preach the gospel: "Go into all the world and preach the gospel..." (Mark 16:15, NKJV). Even this explicit command to them must be applied implicitly to us, though, for it was given not directly to us, but rather to them. Again, we are taught explicitly by example to partake of the Lord's Supper on the first day of the week: Acts 20:7 "On the first day of the week when the disciples came together to break bread..." Once more, even though it was expressed to that first generation of Christians by way of apostolic example,

THE SIMPLE PATTERN 77

nevertheless for us it must be taken implicitly that it applies to us as well.

Even in that generation, though, some things were taught implicitly the first time around. For example, when Philip preached about baptism to the Ethiopian treasurer of Candace, we can only know that this practice was taught directly by an indirect or implicit means. There is no direct mention of his having preached baptism, yet when they came to a certain body of water, the Eunuch appealed to Philip with the words, "See, here is water, what doth hinder me from being baptized?" (Acts 8:35-36, KJV). We may ascertain that baptism was taught, but we cannot know it explicitly.

In the same way, the conversion of the Philippian jailer testifies to the necessity of water baptism (Acts 16:30-33, ASV). This fellow was told in answer to his inquiry ("Sirs, what must I do to be saved?"), "Believe on the Lord Jesus, and thou shalt be saved, thou and thy house?" In verse 32 the Word of the Lord was further spoken to them, and in verse 33 the text declares that he was "baptized, he and all his, immediately." Was baptism preached to him and his family? Of course it was. How do we know, explicitly or implicitly? Indisputably there is no mention directly of baptism being preached, but it is implied by the action taken by himself and his family. They would not have submitted to water baptism if it had not been taught to them.

2) Implicit teaching is just as binding as teaching that is explicit in nature.

God's Word is truth whether it is taught explicitly or implicitly: "Sanctify them through thy truth, thy word is truth" (John 17:17, ASV). "Thy law is truth" (Ps. 119:142, ASV). The truth must be obeyed (1 Pet. 1:22), no matter the format in which it is expressed. As human beings we ought to appreciate this fact, because it applies in every other aspect of life. Why would it not apply in the spiritual realm? If a student were told by his teacher, "Remain in your seat until I come back to the room;" this would imply that he was not to go down the hallway, he was not to go to the office, he was not to go to the restroom, he was not to go across the hall to the classroom where his girlfriend was sitting, etc. Implicit within that order was the exclusion of every conceivable alternative to "remaining in his seat." What is implicit is every bit as important as what is explicit within any given statement. We could in fact multiply the number of examples in the Bible by the hundreds to illustrate the point of this.

3) The silence of the Scriptures is a very important aspect of implicit instruction.

God did not explicitly state that no one from the tribe of Judah could serve as a priest. What he did do was to authorize the tribe of Levi to serve in that capacity. Further, he illustrated through the case of Uzzah that he meant what he said when he gave this authority to the tribe of Levi and thus to none other. The Hebrew writer, in his treatment of this subject, duly noted the importance of divine silence in the program of understanding the authority of Scripture. This principle is simple and understandable. No human being of average intelligence should be able to argue this point from the perspective of ignorance. Hundreds of ordinary illustrations could be marshaled to our cause in supporting this presumption.

Suppose, if you will, that you went into a very expensive restaurant. You noticed immediately the extravagant prices of those things listed on the menu, and considered dutifully that you would be able to afford only one of the entrées. So, you ordered it with a glass of water. Immediately afterward, the waiter came in and placed a very expensive platter of food in front of you from the "appetizer" section of the menu -- which you did not order. "This must be complimentary," you thought to yourself. Also, he brought in a very expensive-looking bottle of wine with a wine goblet for you. The entrée finally arrives at the table, and shortly afterward two side plates of vegetables that you did not order, and to cap it all off, a beautiful dessert (suitable for a king, and with a price-tag to match). At last, he brings the bill. The bottom line is that not only did you receive enough food to feed an entire family, but you were billed for every item delivered to your table, at a cost that would feed a family for a whole week! Do not tell us that you would not complain that you had not ordered all of this stuff or that you would simply hand him your credit card and consider it a lesson in poor choices of restaurants! You would quickly set the waiter straight on what you had ordered and thus, what you intend to pay for. Waiters are not at liberty to bring their customers whatever they want to give them. They must deliver to their table only what they have ordered. Their silence regarding costly bottles of wine, expensive appetizers, and pricey desserts is sufficient to denote that they have no desire for any of those things.

This is not a foreign element with regard to the fundamentals of logical thought. The same thing holds true for the Constitution of these United States of America. In battling the liberal-minded partisans of our time who wish to inject their own modern way of thinking into a two centuries old document, as it were, "between the lines" of the original Constitution, Constitutionalist scholars make the case for the "original intent of the Founders" in much the same way as we do as we approach the Bible. Here are two quotations from a modern legal brief that illustrate the identical point. Aside from the legalese and the case law citations, the reasoning is virtually indistinguishable from what we do when we interpret the Bible:

> "That the Constitution contains no express provision on the subject is not in itself controlling; for with the Constitution...**what is reasonably implied is as much a part of it as what is expressed.**"[17]

> The language of the Constitution **"has to be interpreted in the light of the tacit assumptions upon which it is reasonable to suppose that the language was used."**[18]

---

17 Dillon v. Gloss, 256 U.S. 368, 373 (1921)

18 Ohio ex rel. Popovici v. Agler, 280 U.S. 379, 383 (1930)

> "[W]e must...place ourselves in the position of the men who framed and adopted the Constitution, and inquire what they must have understood to be the meaning and scope of [its provisions]."[19]

The prohibitory significance of God's silence is also deducible from a whole host of scriptures. None is more straightforward in this regard than 2 Timothy 3:16-17, which affirms that the man of God is fully equipped "for every good work" by the "holy scripture." Everything therefore that is not mentioned in the Scriptures would not be qualified in an appropriate delineation of a "good work." Call it what you will, but God's written communication does not permit it to have that description on God's terms. Since the work and worship of the church is so often at the center of this sort of reasoning, it would be fitting and proper to conclude that if a thing is not found in the Bible's narrative of the early church working and worshiping, then it simply has no place at all in today's church. It is without authority and cannot be a "good work."

The principle illustrated here is, of course, applicable to the question of the usage of mechanical instrumental music in the worship of the New Testament church. Some argue that the Bible does not say not to use it. That is of course true, in a direct sense. But what the Bible does say excludes any musical worship other than singing (Eph. 5:19; Col. 3:16). Others would argue that the Bible does not say not to use prayer beads, incense, a separate priesthood, vestments and special robes, *ad infinitum*. Some among our brethren have begun more recently to argue identically when it comes to such matters as the financial support of institutional homes of various types (orphans, widows, the aged) and colleges from the treasury of the local church, the sponsoring church cooperatives, church recreational and entertainment activities, and a coterie of even more radical notions. The point is this: *God does not have to tell us what not to do, only what we ought to do. That is enough.*

---

19 South Carolina v. United States, 199 U.S. 437, 450 (1905). Accord, Ex parte Bain, 121 U.S. 1, 12 (1887)

But who are you, O man, to answer back to God? Will what is molded say to its molder, "Why have you made me like this?" Has the potter no right over the clay, to make out of the same lump one vessel for honorable use and another for dishonorable use? (Rom. 9:20-21, ESV)

Saved by Grace through Faith; Yet Not Without Law

At the outset of this particular part of the discussion, I would like to cite three passages from the New Testament; since understanding and appreciating what they proclaim is very basic to comprehending the major point we are attempting to make:

> For the **grace of God** that bringeth salvation hath appeared to all men, **Teaching us** that, denying ungodliness and worldly lusts, we should live soberly, righteously, and godly, in this present world; Looking for that blessed hope, and the glorious appearing of the great God and our Savior Jesus Christ; Who gave himself for us, that he might redeem us from all iniquity, and purify unto himself a peculiar people, zealous of good works. These things speak, and exhort, and rebuke with all authority. Let no man despise thee (Titus 2:11-15, KJV).

This text says that grace teaches us important spiritual lessons that must not be ignored. Grace is, of course, divine approval or "favor." We are "favored" by God for the work that needs doing. We are not merely "favored" in order to exist in a state of "favoritism" but "favored" in order to accomplish spiritual tasks. Israel was chosen by God to be "a light to the nations" (Isa. 49:6; 60:3) but she failed in that endeavor. God's people (the church) today are to be salt and light to the world (Matt. 5:13-16); we had better not fail in our mission! The consequences are too dire both for ourselves and for the world.

> And now, brethren, I commend you to God, and to the word of his grace, which is able to build you up, and to give you an inheritance among all them which are sanctified (Acts 20:32, KJV).

God's "word of grace" is a message that must be heeded, for it is "able to" build us up into the persons and corporations of Christians that the Lord wants us to be, and ultimately it is "able to" provide for us an inheritance among all those who are set apart for that heavenly home to which we all aspire.

> But **by the grace of God I am what I am**: and his grace which was bestowed upon me was not in vain; **but I labored more abundantly than they all**: yet not I, but the grace of God which was with me (1 Cor. 15:10, KJV).

Paul understood the nature of grace, for no one among the Christian writers wrote about it more forthrightly and circumspectly than did he. But he apparently never got the "memo" that proclaimed that work was not essential to Christian living. Those who are pressing for a "new hermeneutic" for a new age neglect such texts as this one, for it appears to teach a grace that requires a spiritual "work ethic." There is no dispute that Christianity is primarily a grace-faith religious system. There is no denying this, even though sometimes we are portrayed as a people who do not understand this fact, or else a people who deny it outright. This is a brazen misrepresentation. We do, however, reject the denominational idea that comprehends grace as a ticket to heaven without any effort on our part. That is not the prevailing idea that the New Testament promotes, even though it is very popular among certain theologians and a host of preachers who have bought into it with a total investment of heart and mind.

What we glean from reading the New Testament documents is a theology which necessitates counterbalancing notions: that it is at the same time not a legal-works system where the merit is human and the reward is "pay for work performed," while expecting that those who accept the divine favor through their faith will respond to God's mercy and compassion on our sinful state by walking in the Spirit rather than in the flesh (Rom. 8:5-7, 10, 13—"for if you live after the flesh, you shall die"). In Christianity the merit is Christ's and the reward is a gift. Make no mistake about it. But obedience to divine law is expected in its wake. The Bible teaches this in no uncertain terms:

> For **by grace are ye saved through faith**; and that not of yourselves: **it is the gift of God: Not of works**, lest any man should boast. For we are his workmanship, created in Christ Jesus **unto good works**, which God hath before ordained that we should walk in them (Eph 2:8-10, KJV).

> **Being justified freely by his grace** through the redemption that is in Christ Jesus: whom God set forth to be a propitiation, through faith, in his blood, to show his righteousness because of the passing over of the sins done aforetime, in the forbearance of God; for the showing, I say, of his righteousness at this present season: that he might himself be just, and **the justifier of him that hath faith in Jesus**. Where then is the glorying? It is excluded. By what manner of law? of works? Nay: but **by a law of faith** (Rom. 3:24-27, ASV).

God expects that our lives will be characterized by "good works" even though we are saved by grace. And he expects that we will conduct our lives according to a "law of faith" even though the old Law of Moses has come to fulfillment and replacement in Christ. These things being true, there are several facts that need to be considered:

A. Divine Law Has Not Ceased Either To Exist Or Be Enforced

Some people seem to ignore the fact that the terminology of law is still present throughout the New Testament, even with the passing of the old law of Moses. A few citations would be helpful in establishing this proposition:

> There is therefore now no condemnation to them that are in Christ Jesus. For **the law of the Spirit of life in Christ Jesus** made me free from the law of sin and of death. For what the law could not do, in that it was weak through the flesh, God, sending his own Son in the

likeness of sinful flesh and for sin, condemned sin in the flesh: **that the ordinance of the law might be fulfilled in us, who walk not after the flesh, but after the Spirit** (Rom. 8:1-4, ASV).

Then hath he said, Lo, I am come to do thy will. He taketh away the first, **that he may establish the second** (Heb. 10:9, ASV; "the first" had covenant obligations, so does "the second"; yet this fact is often ignored).

Bear ye one another's burdens, and so **fulfill the law of Christ** (Gal 6:2, ASV).

But he that looks into **the perfect law**, the **law of liberty**, and so continueth, being not a hearer that forgets but a **doer that works**, this man shall be **blessed in his doing** (James 1:25, ASV).

With law comes obligation; this cannot be denied, even though it is a law of liberty (freedom from sin and from Moses' system), of life and of love. The language of law, of commandment, of positive affirmation and prohibition, of reward and punishment, of the will of God breached and violated -- all of these things persist in the vocabulary of the New Testament writers even though the Law of Moses has been abrogated. We are no less "under law to Christ" than the previous generations were under law to Moses:

And to the Jews I became as a Jew, that I might gain Jews; to them that are under the law, as under the law, not being myself under the law, that I might gain them that are under the law; to them that are without law, as without law, **not being without law to God**, but **under law to Christ**, that I might gain them that are without law. (1 Cor. 9:20-21, ASV).

Consider for a moment, if you will, the very fact of sin for Christians in the New Testament (cf. 1 John 1:7, 9-10; 2:1-2). Sin is, by definition, a "transgression of the law" (1 John 3:4), or the practice of "lawlessness" *(anomia).* What "law" does this definition involve? Plainly it is not the Law of Moses. And just as plainly it must of necessity be the "law of Christ." So, the very fact of sin and the nature of its definition implies that in the Christian dispensation we are under some form of law, regardless of whether some people like to admit it or not.

B. Saving Grace Is Enjoyed Through An Active Faith

Salvation is never earned; it is the gift of God, not provided because of human merit but because of God's mercy and forgiveness provided in the death of Jesus at the cross. This is true under any and every legal system. Man has proven himself a persistent and even habitual sinner, completely beyond perfection outside of Christ (1 John 1:7, 10). Whatever legal system might ever be devised would lead only to disappointment and failure, so grace is our only hope for deliverance for our sin sickness:

> Being therefore **justified by faith**, we have peace with God through our Lord Jesus Christ; through whom also **we have had our access by faith into this grace** wherein we stand; and we rejoice in hope of the glory of God (Rom. 5:1-2, ASV).

Saving grace is found in Christ and him alone; all spiritual blessing are granted in Christ (Eph. 1:3):

> Therefore I endure all things for the elect's sake, that they also may obtain the **salvation which is in Christ Jesus** with eternal glory. (2 Tim. 2:10, ASV)

> Being justified freely by his grace through the **redemption that is in Christ Jesus**. (Rom. 3:24, ASV)

But saving grace is not by grace or faith alone: God has provided it for the lost to benefit by it; but he will not force it on any of us. We might provide warmth and clothing for a man during a blizzard; but if he does not come in out of the storm and put on the warm clothing, he may well freeze to death, in spite of all the helpful provision that has been made available to him. We may provide food and water to a man who is starving, but if he does not eat the food or drink the water, he will perish. The generosity and kindness of another does not guarantee the sanity or reasonableness of the potential recipient. Every year hundreds of the "homeless" people in America freeze to death in the winter, die of heat exhaustion in the blazing heat of summer, or perish for lack of medical care or other reasons, simply because they refuse to accept the generous provision of society in some shape or form.

Likewise, God has made provision for our deliverance from sin and its terrible consequences, but if we fail to act on our own behalf, we will perish in spite of the amazing generosity and mercy of God. He expects for us to respond to his generous gift with grace and gratitude. All he receives in return from many people is neglect, disregard, carelessness, and even outright animosity. This must not be our reaction to his offering of mercy and compassion:

> So then, my beloved, even as ye have always obeyed, not as in my presence only, but now much more in my absence, **work out your own salvation with fear and trembling; for it is God who worketh in you both to will and to work**, for his good pleasure. (Phil. 2:12-13, ASV)

Men from every nation under the heaven must come to the Lord under the identical terms of pardon and release; there are no exceptions:

> And Peter opened his mouth and said, Of a truth I perceive that God is no respecter of persons: but in every nation **he that fears him, and works righteousness, is acceptable to him**. (Acts 10:34-35, ASV)

C. Passive Faith Is Empty and Will Not Save

Passivity is a bane to the human condition whenever and wherever an emergency condition is the case. Many of us remember the historic explosion of Mount St. Helens on May

18, 1980. It was clear to everyone that unusual activity was taking place under the mountain previous to the eruption, because in the two months before that more than 10,000 small earthquakes had rumbled from below. Those who lived in the area were warned that danger might be ahead. When that day finally arrived, the volcanic blast travelled over 300 miles per hour across the landscape, causing mudslides and tremendous devastation, killing 57 people, some of whom lived miles away from the mountain. Rescue workers had gone door to door to warn people who were close to the rumbling mountain to leave until the danger had passed. But many would not listen because they had felt tremors from below so often over the years that they had grown accustomed to them and were no longer fearful. It is not wise to be passive when action is called for!

James stated the case for it perfectly, so that it cannot be misunderstood:

> What doth it profit, my brethren, if a man say he hath faith, **but have not works**? can that faith save him? If a brother or sister be naked and in lack of daily food, and one of you say unto them, Go in peace, be ye warmed and filled; and yet ye give them not the things needful to the body; what doth it profit? **Even so faith, if it have not works, is dead in itself.** Yea, a man will say, Thou hast faith, and I have works: show me thy faith apart from thy works, and I by my works will show thee my faith. Thou believest that God is one; thou doest well: the demons also believe, and shudder. But wilt thou know, O vain man, that **faith apart from works is barren**? (James 2:14-20, ASV)

This is so because even faith in a sense qualifies as a "work." It is something that we either do or do not do. At any rate, however, it is a thoroughly human action on our side of the equation:

> They said therefore unto him, What must we do, that we may work the works of God? Jesus answered and said unto them, **This is the work of God, that ye believe**

on him whom he hath sent. (John 6:28-29, ASV)

Passive, empty faith is worthless; only faith that responds to God's requirements will deliver the soul, not because the action is meritorious but because the Lord demands it:

> Ye see that **by works a man is justified**, and not only by faith. (James 2:24, ASV)

It must not be forgotten that the gospel was made known unto the obedience of faith for all the nations:

> Through whom we received grace and apostleship, **unto obedience of faith** among all the nations, for his name's sake. (Rom. 1:5, ASV)

> Now to him that is able to establish you according to my gospel and the preaching of Jesus Christ, according to the revelation of the mystery which hath been kept in silence through times eternal, but now is manifested, and by the scriptures of the prophets, according to the commandment of the eternal God, is made known unto all the nations **unto obedience of faith**. (Rom. 16:25-26, ASV)

Passive inactivity is not the response demanded by God: remember the people of ancient Sodom. Lot did not himself at first want to go, for the text says, "But he lingered" (Gen. 19:16, ASV). When he hesitated, the angels "seized him and his wife and his two daughters by the hand...and brought them out." The sons-in-law of the feckless Lot stayed when warned to leave, and they died in the horrendous conflagration when the city was destroyed.

D. Saving Grace and Divine Law Are Inseparable

Remember where we started this part of the discussion? According to Titus 2:11-14, God's saving grace instructs us or "teaches us." It tells us what to deny, how to live, and that for which we should look. It informs us what to speak, exhort and reprove. Furthermore, we are to live by the law of faith:

Then what becomes of our boasting? It is excluded. **By what kind of law?** By a law of works? No, but **by the law of faith**. (Rom. 3:27, ESV)

All of us should remember the Lord's most notable figure portrayed in his public teaching: the concept of the "kingdom of God" or "kingdom of heaven." We must not forget that we follow a king, who has a kingdom ("a ruled people," us), and as such it follows his rule or law:

> And in the days of those kings shall the God of heaven set up a kingdom which shall never be destroyed, nor shall the sovereignty thereof be left to another people; but it shall break in pieces and consume all these kingdoms, and it shall stand for ever. (Dan. 2:44, ASV)

The people of God should be an obedient people. If we are not, then we are a "disobedient people" as Israel of old proved to be, and recall that this did not turn out too well for them (Rom. 10:21). Stressing the keeping God's commandments may seem to some people to be mere "legalism," but we will rest in the surety of the witness of Holy Scripture to the will of God on this count:

> And hereby we know that we know him, **if we keep his commandments. He that saith, I know him, and keepeth not his commandments, is a liar, and the truth is not in him; but whoso keepeth his word, in him verily hath the love of God been perfected**. Hereby we know that we are in him: he that saith he abideth in him ought himself also to walk even as he walked. Beloved, no new commandment write I unto you, but an old commandment which ye had from the beginning: the old commandment is the word which ye heard. (1 John 2:3-7, ASV)

> **And why call ye me, Lord, Lord, and do not the things which I say?** (Luke 6:46, ASV)

And he was told, "Your mother and your brothers are standing outside, desiring to see you." But he answered

> them, "**My mother and my brothers are those who hear the word of God and do it.**" (Luke 8:20-21, ESV)

> Seeing ye have purified your souls in **your obedience to the truth** unto unfeigned love of the brethren, love one another from the heart fervently. (1 Pet. 1:22, ASV)

> But thanks be to God, that, whereas ye were servants of sin, **ye became obedient from the heart to that form of teaching whereunto ye were delivered**; and being made free from sin, ye became servants of righteousness. (Rom. 6:17-18, ASV)

In the face of all this, we are told by many in our generation that obedience is not necessary, at least in the form of strict compliance with the divine will revealed to us in the teachings of the New Testament. We are further informed that it is mere legalism to preach obedience to the Bible. In reality, their theory represents nothing short of lawlessness, which is repeatedly condemned as sin in the Scriptures. As the Lord himself said regarding the judgment of the wicked: "And then will I declare to them, 'I never knew you; depart from me, you workers of lawlessness'" (*anomia*, Matt. 7:23). And, as the Apostle John warned the sometimes brutish Gnostics and their followers:

> Everyone who makes a practice of sinning also practices lawlessness *(anomia)*; **sin is lawlessness.** You know that he appeared to take away sins, and in him there is no sin. **No one who abides in him keeps on sinning; no one who keeps on sinning has either seen him or known him**. Little children, let no one deceive you. Whoever practices righteousness is righteous, as he is righteous. **Whoever makes a practice of sinning is of the devil**, for the devil has been sinning from the beginning. The reason the Son of God appeared was to destroy the works of the devil. **No one born of God makes a practice of sinning**, for God's seed abides in him, and he cannot keep on sinning because he has been born of God. (1 John 3:4-9, ESV)

Our salvation by God's grace is contingent on both our faith in Christ and our ongoing obedience to the gospel of Christ: "Although he was a son, he learned obedience through what he suffered. And being made perfect, **he became the source of eternal salvation to all who obey him**" (Heb. 5:8-9, ESV). There is no promise of good things to evil doers who do not repent and change their way of living. Persistent sin is a destroyer, even in the shadow of the cross.

Does the New Testament Possess "Pattern Authority"?

Paul instructed Timothy not to be careless with his words, but rather to see them as shaping both the present and the future. Words are powerful things and they must not be thrown about with ruthless abandon:

> **Hold the pattern of sound words** which thou hast heard from me, in faith and love which is in Christ Jesus. (2 Tim. 1:13, ASV)

They, as it were, sculpt the thinking of their hearers. So, retaining a proper sense of what has gone before, especially with regard to what has been spoken by the apostles, must be a constant consideration for those who care about the fidelity of self and others to the truth:

> But, beloved, **remember ye the words which were spoken before of the apostles** of our Lord Jesus Christ. (Jude 17, KJV)

From very ancient times there were enemies of the notion that there existed an objective standard in many areas, such as morals and religion. The ancient Sophists were accustomed to saying, "Every man is a measure unto himself." One philosopher of the sophistic orientation, Protagoras (490-420 B.C.), set forth a version of this observation which was considered to be subversive at the time, but which has become quite popular with many moderns, "Man is the measure of all things: of things which are, that they are, and of things which are not, that they are not." By this he meant that truth is relative to the person who entertains it. He believed in the relativity of all judgments to the experience or belief of the individual making the judgment, i.e. what we would today call, "subjectivism." On that interpretation, the way things seem to an individual is the way they are in fact for that individual. For someone else, it might be quite different, for it may appear differently to them. He was also a proponent of agnosticism. By the way, these two philosophical inclinations, agnosticism and subjectivism, tend to fit "hand in glove." The Christian who begins to incline in the direction of subjectivism must be very careful that he does not ultimately lean also toward its bosom friend, agnosticism.

Socrates agreed to Protagoras' main contention about the relativity of things, and even argued it this way: he said that if the wind feels cold to me and warm to you, then it is cold for me and warm for you. In the course of his dialogue, Socrates expanded the thesis to apply to all judgments, yielding the result that every belief is true for the person who holds it (and only for them), and hence there is no objective truth on any matter. Today we would respond that there is a mode for checking the true temperature, and it is called a thermometer. What it yields is an objective measurement of the temperature. If the thermometer reads 72 degrees, it matters little what our subjective "feeling" about it may be, for the objective standard has declared a precise reading of the real ambient temperature, and all other guesses and speculations are simply beside the point. A true objective standard is possible and may be utilized to judge the accuracy of all such alternatives.

Those who today are so busily engaged in attacking the notion of the Bible possessing "pattern authority" are telling us virtually the same thing as these ancient philosophers promoted: "All truth is relative; God has no hard and fast rules; make up your own, as it pleases you." They have bought into a form of illogical relativism. In the course of doing so, they have also rejected the objective standard of measurement: the Bible as the Word of God.

A. What do we mean by "pattern"?

When we utilize this term, it is not something we have

invented. It is a Bible term and it expresses a thoroughly biblical idea. Patterns tell us what God wills. You might say that patterns are rather like "blueprints" for our beliefs and our actions. The blueprint for a house shows how it should be built. A blueprint for a car would inform us how it should be constructed. A blueprint for a boat would in all likelihood show the size and shape of the hull, how the deck is to be constructed, what rigging would be included, etc.

The blueprint would not show us all of the details, however; but it would include some. It probably would not tell us the brick color of a house, might not include the paint color of a car, likely would not give engine specifications for an outboard motor (whether 100, 150, 200, 250 horsepower; whether Evinrude, Johnson or Mercury). But sometimes it might: we would not want to own an underpowered car or an underpowered boat, so we might specify a minimum standard for either one; and we would need enough heat and cooling power in a house to keep it warm in the winter and cool in the summer, so once more there might need to be a stated HVAC minimum in the specifications of the pattern. Those who teach that a biblical pattern exists do not require that every specific is given in order to establish a pattern. A pattern will be just as generic as God sometimes is, and just as specific as God sometimes is. It would be a mistake, though, to conclude that God is never interested in specifics or details. The Bible teaches otherwise.

God was sometimes very concerned with details, while at other times he left some things to the discretion of men. Here are a few cases where he defined specifically what he had in mind, and by doing so, meant to leave out anything else:

1) Dimensions of the ark (Gen. 6:15= 300x50x30 cubits)

2) Type of fire offered by Nadab and Abihu (Lev. 10:1)

3) Exactness of the building of the tabernacle (Ex. 25:40; Heb. 8:5)

4) Who was allowed to touch the ark of the covenant (1

Chron. 13:10)

The text that we began this section with, 2 Timothy 1:13, deals with the "pattern" *(tupōsin)* of "sound words" in gospel teaching and preaching. We may imply from this that if there is "sound" teaching which results from "sound words," then logically there is "unsound" teaching which is caused or enabled by "unsound words." Thus, what follows the pattern is sound, and what fails to do so, or departs from the pattern, is inherently "unsound."

The word *tupos* "form, example, pattern" is found sixteen times in the New Testament. Also, the alternative words *hupodeigma* and *hupotuposis*, are also used and each one is translated, among other terms, as "pattern." The designation, *hupogrammos* (1 Pet. 2:21), is an "under-writing" a writing copy, a writing sample for imitation. These words imply in their various contexts the following meanings:

1) The teaching which embodies the sum and substance of religion and represents it to the mind: Christian teaching as a mould or norm (used in both a moral and doctrinal sense).

2) The pattern in conformity to which a thing must be made.

3) Pattern of teaching.

4) An example to be imitated, a model, a pattern, a scheme, a form, a type, a figure, a system, a form of doctrine.

5) The gospel is a mould; those who are obedient to its teachings become thereby conformed to Christ.

The lives and teachings of early disciples were ordered by a definite and exact doctrine. They considered it "once for all delivered to the saints" (Jude 3, ESV). It was the basis of the lives they lived, the faith they believed, and the practices which they involved themselves in and with. To deny this is to deny the terminology employed so regularly by the writers of the New Testament. These are their words not ours. The Restoration Movement did not invent this language; rather it was borrowed from the documents that comprise the New Testament.

B. Accepting the Pattern Authority of the New Testament Expresses Love for God and Christ; Rejecting Or Ignoring It Evidences Lack of Love

Men cannot respond to a revelation from God amorphously. This is a general truism that is readily illustrated. For example, one cannot respond to his wife amorphously, he must manifest his love for her in material ways (providing for her, protecting her, helping her, showing affection, etc.). In like manner, one cannot respond to a child amorphously, but will necessarily show love in physical and other ways (feeding, caring for, clothing, providing for, showing affection). In this context, the words, "I love you" are empty of meaning unless backed up by actions that prove the words.

Likewise, human beings need some means to demonstrate affection for God; and the Lord has provided for that in every era of his revelation: by the observation of his commands (rules, regulations) in order to manifest outwardly the love of God that is claimed. In every dispensation of history this has been true. It is still just as true today.

In the Old Testament this was linked inextricably with obedience to God's commands. Moses expressed this to the children of Israel thus:

> Know therefore that the LORD your God is God, the faithful God who keeps covenant and **steadfast love with those who love him and keep his commandments**, to a thousand generations, and repays to their face those who hate him, by destroying them. He will not be slack with one who hates him. He will repay him to his face. You shall therefore **be careful to do the commandment and the statutes and the rules that I command you** today. "And because you listen to these rules and keep and do them, the LORD your God will keep with you the covenant and the steadfast love that he swore to your fathers. **He**

> **will love you**, bless you, and multiply you. He will also
> bless the fruit of your womb and the fruit of your
> ground, your grain and your wine and your oil, the
> increase of your herds and the young of your flock, in
> the land that he swore to your fathers to give you (Deut.
> 7:9-13, ESV).

The same thing may be observed in the New Testament. Both
Jesus and John set it forth in language that demonstrates
John's dependence on the instruction of Christ. The Lord said it
first, and then John reiterated it in slightly different
phraseology:

> **If ye love me, ye will keep my
> commandments.** (John 14:15, ASV)

> **If ye keep my commandments, ye shall
> abide in my love**; even as **I have kept my
> Father's commandments, and abide in his
> love.** (John 15:10, ASV)

> Hereby we know that we love the children of
> God, **when we love God and do his
> commandments.** For **this is the love of God,
> that we keep his commandments**: and his
> commandments are not grievous. (1 John 5:2-3,
> ASV)

By what principle of spirituality is it proper to accede to the
devilish notion that one may sincerely and honestly love God
and yet at every whim ignore his commandments or else breach
them with impunity? Such a viewpoint is in no sense biblical or
even Christian. It acquiesces to the "spirit of the age" or
Zeitgeist. That much is certain. But it is at the same time
profoundly antithetical to everything that we may gather from
the divine revelation of God's will for man found in the Book of
Books.

C. The Principle Designator of the Pattern Was and Is the Language "According To..."

In the Old Testament we have become familiar with the language of precise obedience. Several different phrases are utilized to characterize it, but the most persistent one is the expression "according to..." Something comparable to it was present in a whole host of different contexts, although for our purposes its presence in the biblical narratives are too numerous for us to mention even a substantial number of the instances. Below we list a few of them:

> Thus did Noah; **according to all** that God commanded him, so did he. (Gen 6:22, ASV)

> And Noah did **according unto all** that the LORD commanded him. (Gen 7:5, KJV)

> Thus did all the children of Israel; **as the LORD commanded** Moses and Aaron, **so did they**. (Exod. 12:50, KJV)

> **According to all** that the LORD commanded Moses, so the children of Israel made all the work. (Exod. 39:42, KJV)

The story of the Syrian general Naaman is particularly noteworthy, because he at first hesitated in his obedience to the prophet's demand. He no doubt reflected upon the clear, cool waters of his homeland's rivers to the North, the Abana and the Pharpar, and wondered at the idea of dipping himself into the muddy Jordan River, but in the end yielded to the commandment given to him. When he obeyed, and not until he obeyed, his disease was taken away:

> Then went he down, and dipped himself seven times in Jordan, **according to the saying of the man of God**: and his flesh came again like unto the flesh of a little child, and he was clean. (2 Kings 5:14, KJV)

Similar language is found in the New Testament as well; it is indicative that the principle of the necessity of absolute obedience persists into the present era. There is nothing found in the New Testament that suggests that because Jesus has been offered as the Lamb of God "that taketh away the sins of the world," we may henceforth flaunt the Word of God and ignore its sometimes frightening warnings (Rom. 6:1-2; Heb. 10:26ff.; etc). Rather, we must also demonstrate an attitude which shows our desire always to please God and do his bidding in every particular:

> For Moses truly said unto the fathers, A prophet shall the Lord your God raise up unto you of your brethren, like unto me; him shall ye hear in **all things whatsoever he shall say unto you** (cf. Deut. 18:15). And it shall come to pass, that every soul, which will not hear that prophet, shall be destroyed from among the people (Acts 3:22-23, KJV).

> For I bear them record that they have a zeal of God, but **not according to knowledge**. For they being ignorant of God's righteousness, and going about to establish their own righteousness, **have not submitted themselves unto the righteousness of God**. (Rom. 10:2-3, KJV)

> Now the God of patience and consolation grant you to be likeminded one toward another **according to Christ Jesus**. (Rom. 15:5, KJV)

> Now to him that is of power to stablish you according to my gospel, and the preaching of Jesus Christ, **according to the revelation of the mystery, which was kept secret since the world began**. (Rom. 16:25, KJV)

D. How Does the Concept of "Pattern Authority" Apply to Us Today?

The Apostles of Christ organized churches in a certain and definite way, and correctness in doctrine was also emphasized by them. Of course, there were cultural and linguistic variations within those early congregations. And some were quicker learners than others. In point of fact, some showed stubbornness and a tendency to return to their pagan ways. Still, there is a consistency in the apostolic "blueprint" for the church in all of the various cities and towns from Jerusalem to Asia Minor that it is difficult even for the cynical detractor to deny. In addition, they were quick to point out that some had failed to meet the test and had departed from the pattern:

> Now these things, brethren, I have in a figure transferred to myself and Apollos for your sakes; that in us ye might learn **not to go beyond the things which are written**; that no one of you be puffed up for the one against the other. (1 Cor. 4:6, ASV)

> **Whosoever goeth onward and abideth not in the teaching of Christ, hath not God:** he that abideth in the teaching, the same hath both the Father and the Son. If any one cometh unto you, and **bringeth not this teaching, receive him not into your house, and give him no greeting**: for he that giveth him greeting partaketh in his evil works. (2 John 1:9-11, ASV)

Ignorance of or unwillingness to yield oneself to the pattern was seen as an offense to the whole church, and as such was considered proper grounds for shunning their company in order to make them aware of their folly:

> Now I beseech you, brethren, **mark them that are causing the divisions and occasions of stumbling, contrary to the doctrine which ye learned: and turn away from them.** For they that are such serve not our Lord Christ, but their own belly; and by their smooth and fair speech they beguile the hearts of the innocent. For your obedience is come abroad unto all men. I rejoice therefore over you: but I would have you wise unto that which is good, and simple unto that which is evil. (Rom. 16:17-19, ASV)

> Now we command you, brothers, in the name of our Lord Jesus Christ, that you **keep away from any**

> **brother who is walking in idleness and not in accord with the tradition that you received from us.** For you yourselves know how **you ought to imitate us,** because we were not idle when we were with you, nor did we eat anyone's bread without paying for it, but with toil and labor we worked night and day, that we might not be a burden to any of you. It was not because we do not have that right, but to give you in ourselves an example to imitate. For even when we were with you, **we would give you this command: If anyone is not willing to work, let him not eat.** For we hear that some among you walk in idleness, not busy at work, but busybodies. Now such persons we command and encourage in the Lord Jesus Christ to do their work quietly and to earn their own living. (2 Thess. 3:6-12, ESV)

Perversion of gospel teaching was an offense worthy of the most severe condemnation. Paul "anathematized" those who were audacious enough to attempt it. How can we be so bold today as to consider this a mere misdemeanor, when he used such pungent language to censure and denounce it?

> I marvel that ye are so quickly **removing** from him that called you in the grace of Christ **unto a different gospel;** which is not another gospel only there are some that **trouble you,** and **would pervert the gospel of Christ.** But though we, or an angel from heaven, should preach unto you any gospel other than that which we preached unto you, let him be anathema. As we have said before, so say I now again, if any man preacheth unto you any gospel other than that which ye received, **let him be anathema.** For am I now seeking the favor of men, or of God? or am I striving to please men? if I were still pleasing men, I should not be a servant of Christ. For I make known to you, brethren, as touching the gospel which was preached by me, that it is not after man. For neither did I receive it from man, nor was I taught it, but it came to me through revelation of Jesus Christ. (Gal. 1:6-12, ASV)

Sometimes the language of the apostles was very severe and even dissonant (too harsh for modern sensibilities perhaps), in dealing with those who had departed from the faith. I allege that we are not wise enough to "second guess" these men of God who wrote under the inspiration of the Holy Spirit. Apparently the excesses of these deceivers were as bad as they were portrayed to be and thus worthy of the recriminations of inspired men:

> For there are many **unruly men, vain talkers and deceivers**, specially they of the circumcision, **whose mouths must be stopped**; men who **overthrow whole houses, teaching things which they ought not**, for filthy lucre's sake. One of themselves, a prophet of their own, said, Cretans are always liars, evil beasts, idle gluttons. This testimony is true. For which cause **reprove them sharply, that they may be sound in the faith**, not giving heed to Jewish fables, and commandments of men who turn away from the truth. To the pure all things are pure: but to them that are **defiled and unbelieving** nothing is pure; but **both their mind and their conscience are defiled**. They **profess that they know God; but by their works they deny him, being abominable, and disobedient, and unto every good work reprobate**. (Titus 1:10-16, ASV)

If the Bible does not possess pattern authority, as some contend, then it is unavoidable that we should conclude that God intends for us to worship him in any way we see proper, and that we may at every turn ignore altogether those directives that are found in the New Testament.

Furthermore, to say that there is no pattern at all in the Biblical revelation is to say there the Bible is a meaningless book, stands for nothing and has no distinctive teaching whatever. Surely anyone who has read the Bible at all can see that this view is wrong and destructive, leading us nowhere at breakneck speed. It is plainly the offspring of modernistic thinking which in its essence takes the Bible as a thoroughly human book with little or no eternal moral, ethical, or ecclesiastical information for us to learn from it.

J. G. Machen, in his excellent book *Christianity and Liberalism*, observed:

> It is perfectly conceivable that the originators of the Christian movement had no right to legislate for subsequent generations; but at any rate **they did have an inalienable right to legislate for all generations that should choose to bear the name "Christian."** It is conceivable that Christianity may now have to be abandoned, and another religion substituted for it; but at any rate the question of what Christianity is can be determined only by an examination of the beginnings of Christianity. **Christianity is an historical phenomenon and as an historical phenomenon it must be investigated on the basis of historical evidence.**[20]

The only conceivable way we have of understanding Christianity is by a close study of the Christian documents. They are the key to any mystery that might be conceived relative to that movement, its sacred beliefs and practices. If we wish to imitate it in any respect, a close study of the documents is essential, and an adherence to what is learned from that investigation must be applied in every aspect of our religious praxis.

How Did Jesus Establish Authority?

In one intriguing instance, the Lord employed a strengthened form of the word for "interpret" *(diermēneusen)* in Luke 24:27. Jesus *"expounded* to them in all the Scriptures the things concerning Himself":

> And he said to them, "O foolish ones, and slow of heart to believe all that the prophets have spoken! Was it not

---

20 J. G. Machen, *Christianity and Liberalism* (Grand Rapids: Wm. B. Eerdmans, 1923), 20-21.

necessary that the Christ should suffer these things and enter into his glory?" And beginning with Moses and all the Prophets, **he interpreted** to them in all the Scriptures the things concerning himself (Luke 24:25-27, ESV).

This is a word that refers to the common sense principles by which we interpret, explain or expound the Scriptures. In fact, we utilize practically the same ones to interpret our Constitution, and for that matter, all written communications. The word *hermeneutics* means "the art or science of the interpretation of literature."[21] The Greek word *hermeneuō* is defined as, "(cf. Hermes, the name of the pagan god Mercury, who was regarded as the messenger of the gods), denotes to explain, interpret (Eng., hermeneutics)."[22] At first, the word had no special reference to Scripture. It represented a formal or informal set of literary techniques for reading and understanding any literature.

Those who in our own day are calling for us to employ a new hermeneutic, or way of interpreting and applying the NT are saying they do not believe the methods of interpretation we have used in the past are correct. They inform us that the idea of interpreting and applying Scripture to our lives by means of precept, example and necessary inference should be discarded and we should look for some other more modernistic way of understanding Biblical authority.

Some also say that we should "study the life of Jesus and do what we feel he would do in the situation." It seems strange to us that people who profess to follow Jesus would suggest a standard that he neither suggested nor exemplified. They would turn us away from Holy Scripture as our only guide and pattern for life and turn us toward something that they deem more fitting. If we are to follow the example of Jesus, surely

---

21 Webster.

22 W.E. Vine, Merrill F. Unger and William White, Jr., "Interpret, Interpretation, Interpreter," In *Vine's Complete Expository Dictionary of Old and New Testament Words* (Nashville, TN: T. Nelson, 1996).

that would include following his example in how to establish God's Biblical authority, that is, the way he interpreted and applied the Bible to modern life.

It is noteworthy to us that Jesus always went to Scripture as his first line of defense of the truth. For example, in every temptation of Jesus, He appealed to the written word of God. He did not quote the ordinary words of uninspired men, but cited the words of the Hebrew Bible, the sacred book held in common by all of the Jews. When the devil said, "If you are the Son of God, command that these stones become bread," Jesus responded, "**It is written**, Man shall not live by bread alone, but by every word that proceeds from the mouth of God" (Matt. 4:3-4, NKJV).

When the tempter quoted Scripture (Ps. 91:11-12), Jesus countered once more by saying, "**It is written again**, You shall not tempt the Lord your God" (Matt. 4:7, NKJV). To the third temptation, Jesus exclaimed, "Away with you Satan! For **it is written**, You shall worship the Lord your God, and him only you shall serve" (Matt. 4:10, NKJV).

> If we can understand anything at all about the example of Jesus from what is revealed to us in the written Gospels, he taught us to act only by the authority of God, to accept everything he said, and to trust him implicitly as he guides us through the medium of Sacred Scripture. To our mind, that does not in any way cause us to lean in the direction of some subjective feeling of what God *might* want us to do in a certain situation.

A. Jesus Used Precepts (Commands Or Statements Of Fact From Scripture) As Authoritative.

When our Lord was asked about the Father's will by a certain lawyer who wanted to know what to do to inherit eternal life, he responded by saying, "What is written in the law? What is your reading of it?" (Luke 10:26, NKJV). The lawyer in turn quoted God's words as revealed through Moses, and Jesus said, "You have answered rightly, do this and you will live" (v. 28, NKJV).

At another time, when the Pharisees asked Him about whether a man had the right to divorce his wife over every conceivable cause, he quoted Genesis 2:24 and concluded, "Therefore what God has joined together, let not man separate" (Matt. 19:6, NKJV). The Pharisees objected to his application of that passage and tried to circumvent this particular interpretation of it by appealing to what Moses permitted, but Jesus insisted that the statement of Genesis 2:24 included both explicit and implicit truth, and thus it revealed God's intention for men, even many hundreds of years after it had been written.

B. Jesus Appealed To Examples In The Bible (Old Testament) And Taught His Disciples To Follow Them.

Certain scribes and Pharisees asked Jesus to show them other signs than the ones he had already performed. Apparently they were not satisfied with what they had seen and heard to that point, but this did not deter him at all. Instead, he cited certain instances and examples from the Bible to illustrate his point:

> An evil and adulterous generation seeks after a sign, and no sign will be given to it except the sign of the prophet Jonah. For as Jonah was three days and three nights in the belly of the great fish, so will the Son of Man be three days and three nights in the heart of the earth. The men of Nineveh will rise in the judgment with this generation and condemn it, because they repented at the preaching of Jonah; and indeed a greater than Jonah is here. The queen of the South will rise up in the judgment with this generation and condemn it, for she came from the ends of the earth to hear the wisdom of Solomon, and indeed a greater than Solomon is here. (Matt. 12:29-32, NKJV)

In this passage Jesus used examples (Jonah, Nineveh, and King Solomon and his meeting with the Queen of Sheba) to convince them that they needed to listen to His teaching! The story of the famous reluctant prophet Jonah was located in the Minor Prophets. The particular lesson he pointed to from the great city Nineveh was recited in the book of Jonah. The summit that took place between the Queen of Sheba and

Israel's wisest king Solomon is also recorded in the Old Testament. This pagan ruler went away greatly marveling at the wisdom that God had bestowed on the Israelite monarch (1 Kings 10:4-9).

In still another case, after demonstrating his personal humility, in the washing of His disciples' feet, Jesus said,

> "If I then, your Lord and Teacher, have washed your feet, you also ought to wash one another's feet" (John 13:14, NKJV).

Not only did the Lord provide them with an example, he commanded them to follow it!

Those who say we do not learn from examples are not following the example of Jesus. In fact, even many of the commands in Scripture come to us through examples. In a good many instances they were given to someone else originally, and we are led to conclude that they apply to us also:

> Go therefore and make disciples of all nations, baptizing them in the name of the Father and of the Son and of the Holy Spirit, (20) teaching them to observe all that I have commanded you. And behold, I am with you always, to the end of the age" (Matt. 28:19-20; ESV).

Although the original command was given to the apostles, their duty to share the message of the resurrected and glorified Christ was understood by them as they were forced from their homes into a new Diaspora of their own:

> They therefore that were scattered abroad, went about preaching the word. (Acts 8:4, ASV)

C. Jesus Established Authority Through The Use Of Necessary Inference From Scripture.

The Sadducees thought they had Jesus on the horns of a dilemma because of the case of a woman who had been married to seven brothers. They had probably used this instance many times previously against the Pharisees. This time they did not go away with a victory in the debate. Jesus responded to their speculation thus:

> You are mistaken, not knowing the Scriptures nor the power of God. For in the resurrection they neither marry nor are given in marriage, but are like angels of God in heaven. But concerning the resurrection of the dead, have you not read what was spoken to you by God, saying, I am the God of Abraham, the God of Isaac, and the God of Jacob? God is not the God of the dead, but of the living. (Matt. 22:29-32, NKJV)

The example of God speaking to Moses from the burning bush (Exod. 3:6), necessarily implied that Abraham, Isaac and Jacob continued to exist, therefore the Sadducees were wrong about their doctrine. Jesus did not hesitate to draw a conclusion from what was an implication from the text.

Again, at the end of the identical chapter, Jesus drew a necessary inference from David's statement, "The Lord said to my Lord, Sit on My right hand, Till I make Your enemies Your footstool" (Matt. 22:44, NKJV; Ps. 110:1). He concluded from this simple remark that, "If David then calls Him Lord, how is He his Son?" (Matt. 22:45, NKJV). They had no answer, because they could not deny the necessary implication in the Scripture. David had called someone his Lord, and claimed Jehovah God had addressed him; this they could not refute! Yes, we should follow the example of Jesus in every possible way, but that should include His example of respect for precept, example and necessary inference. He used all three in his teachings, and to excellent effect.

Jesus never told anyone, ever, to study the life of Moses and do what he felt Moses would do under his own new set of circumstances. Rather, he quoted precepts and examples from God's word and drew necessary conclusions from the words of Sacred Writ. Those who say that today all we need do is study the life of Jesus and simply do whatever we feel he would do under similar circumstances, are not really following Jesus. They are instead following the leadings of their own heart, and ignoring the fact that the human heart is extremely corrupt, and often given to following and gratifying (in one way or another) its own lusts and then justifying them with specious arguments:

> There is a way which seemeth right unto a man, But the end thereof are the ways of death. (Prov. 16:25, ASV)

> Thus says the LORD: "Cursed is the man who trusts in man and makes flesh his strength, whose heart turns away from the LORD. (6) He is like a shrub in the desert, and shall not see any good come. He shall dwell in the parched places of the wilderness, in an uninhabited salt land. (7) "Blessed is the man who trusts in the LORD, whose trust is the LORD. (8) He is like a tree planted by water, that sends out its roots by the stream, and does not fear when heat comes, for its leaves remain green, and is not anxious in the year of drought, for it does not cease to bear fruit." (9) **The heart is deceitful above all things, and desperately sick; who can understand it?** (10) "I the LORD search the heart and test the mind, to give every man according to his ways, according to the fruit of his deeds" (Jer. 17:5-10, NKJV)

How Did the Apostles Establish Authority?

The Lord's apostles adhered to the pattern of Christ in their own practice of carefully following God's Word. They did so by accepting divine statements as fact, by respecting and obeying divine commandments, by using examples as a means for determining God's will, and by the employment of inference, or "drawing conclusions from a premise" as a means of interpreting the words of Christ and of the Holy Scriptures.

A. Divine Statements Were Accepted As Fact.

To the mind of an unbeliever or a modernist "Christian," every statement from the Bible is subject to review. It cannot be taken at face value. Unfortunately, down through the years of our history there have arisen different popular personalities who have berated the facts given in the Bible as "unhistorical," "unreliable," and even "unbelievable." One famous instance of this in our history is that of Robert C. Cave (1843-1923), outspoken minister of the Central Christian Church in St. Louis. His conversion to liberal theology was thoroughgoing. From that pulpit he argued that God did not command Abraham to slay his son or require Jephthah to offer his daughter in sacrifice. As regards the New Testament, he denied both the virgin birth and the bodily resurrection of Jesus. He was quickly dismissed from his preaching job, but persisted with his rants in a journal called the *Non-Sectarian*. On those pages he derided the principles of "Christian primitivism," defined sin in terms of ignorance, affirmed the divinity within all people, and labeled the atonement of Christ as a moral outrage.[23]

Similarly, in *Voices of Concern* (to which we alluded earlier), Logan Fox rejected the Bible as the verbally inspired Word of God, and said: "I came to realize that rather than making the Bible alive, the verbal inspiration theory was killing the message of the Bible."[24] Cecil Franklin confessed, "I did not have the feeling of personal security to enable me to speak freely of my doubts and growing disbeliefs.[25]" N. L. Parks rejected Bible authority altogether, making the case for personal subjectivism: "The free man questions, tries, tests. He acknowledges no authority to which he does not freely consent as internalized truth. He is subject to no control above his own conscience. He does not obey because he is commanded, but because it is the way of truth and wisdom."[26]

The apostles showed no such inclination toward disbelief. They accepted at face value all of the statements of Holy Scripture. They never once displayed any disparagement of or cynicism about the teachings of the Word of God. Here are a few

---

23 L. A. McAllister, W. A. Tucker, *Journey in Faith: A History of the Christian Church (Disciples of Christ)* (St. Louis: Bethany Press, 1975), 364.

24 Robert Meyers ed., *Voices of Concern* (St. Louis: Mission Messenger, 1966), 19.

25 Ibid., 78.

26 Ibid., 80-81.

illustrations of their complete faith in the integrity and veracity of the Bible:

> And the Holy Spirit also bears witness to us; for after saying, (quoting Jer. 31:31ff.) "This is the covenant that I will make with them after those days, declares the Lord: I will put my laws on their hearts, and write them on their minds," then he adds, "I will remember their sins and their lawless deeds no more" (Heb. 10:15-17; ESV).

> But it is not as though the word of God has failed. For not all who are descended from Israel belong to Israel, and not all are children of Abraham because they are his offspring, but (quoting Gen. 21:12) "Through Isaac shall your offspring be named." This means that it is not the children of the flesh who are the children of God, but the children of the promise are counted as offspring. For this is what the promise said (quoting Gen. 18:10): "About this time next year I will return, and Sarah shall have a son." And not only so, but also when Rebekah had conceived children by one man, our forefather Isaac, though they were not yet born and had done nothing either good or bad--in order that God's purpose of election might continue, not because of works but because of him who calls--she was told (quoting Gen. 25:23), "The older will serve the younger." As it is written, "Jacob I loved, but Esau I hated." What shall we say then? Is there injustice on God's part? By no means! (Rom. 9:6-14, ESV)

We could multiply these quotations by the hundreds. In every instance the Old Testament is quoted as entirely dependable and worthy of the total confidence of the reader. Such folk as cast doubt upon the text, its integrity, its historicity, its authenticity -- simply stated, have lost their faith in the God of the Bible. There is no need to sugar-coat it!

B. God's Commandments Were Respected, Heeded, And Obeyed.

Here we do not have reference to the Ten Commandments, for they were a part of the Law of Moses which was nailed to the cross of Christ (Col. 2:14-17). Rather, we mean to say that the apostles respected, heeded and obeyed all of the commandments of God as they were delivered to them through the Holy Spirit. This comprise the New Covenant of Jesus Christ, or the New Testament. Those who refused to act in accordance with this objective standard of truth were unworthy of the fellowship of the community of faith:

> And we have confidence in the Lord touching you, **that ye both do and will do the things which we command**. And the Lord direct your hearts into the love of God, and into the patience of Christ. **Now we command you, brethren, in the name of our Lord Jesus Christ**, that ye withdraw yourselves from every brother that walketh disorderly, and not after the tradition which they received of us. For yourselves **know how ye ought to imitate us: for we behaved not ourselves disorderly among you**; neither did we eat bread for nought at any man's hand, but in labor and travail, working night and day, that we might not burden any of you: not because we have not the right, but **to make ourselves an example unto you**, that ye should imitate us. For even when we were with you, **this we commanded you**, If any will not work, neither let him eat. For we hear of some that walk among you disorderly, that work not at all, but are busybodies. Now them that are such **we command and exhort** in the Lord Jesus Christ, that with quietness they work, and eat their own bread. But ye, brethren, be not weary in well-doing. **And if any man obeyeth not our word by this epistle**, note that man, that ye have no company with him, to the end that he may be ashamed (2 Thess. 3:4-14, ASV).

C. Biblical Examples Were Honored and Imitated.

On a number of different occasions, Paul calls on the example of "approved practice" in other churches to demonstrate how a congregation should conduct its activities. In I Corinthians 4:17, for instance, Paul tells Timothy he was sent to tell the Corinthians what Paul taught "in every church." His blueprint for the church was consistent everywhere. Again, Paul sought to have a common practice on essential matters as indicated by I Corinthians 14:33b where he says, "as in all the churches, let the women keep silent." This, he says, is the practice of other churches, and he uses this as a basis for arguing that the Corinthian church should do the same. Again, in I Corinthians 16:1, Paul says he wants the Corinthians to follow the instruction he gave to the Galatians about contributing on the first day of the week. Paul, then, used the already approved practice of one congregation as a precedent for others to follow. What the Galatians did, the Corinthians ought to do. Why would we today consider acting any differently, unless we are possessed of a rebellious spirit?

Some of what God wants us to know, then, He has put into example form rather than a command. Now of course, we recognize that we have to use extreme care in interpreting examples. We must ask some questions as we do so. Does this example present an abiding and eternal principle or one restricted to a particular circumstance or even a different dispensation? Is the practice merely incidental to the main lesson of the text, or is it clearly intended to present a lasting principle for every age of men to follow? What were the circumstances which prevailed that might affect our following the example?

Yet, that God has used the example method of revealing what he wants us to do is clearly established by apostolic decree. Just as he used commands and direct statements to instruct us of his will, he also makes use of "approved practice" as a means of delivering his will to us.

D. Necessary Inferences From Scripture Were Used And Bound On Disciples of Christ As Divine Law.

As regards this subject, let me say another word or two about the nature of inference, for it would be difficult to overstate the opposition that this method has with some detractors. Inference means drawing a conclusion from what has been implied in a statement. The validity of the conclusion, of course, depends both on the strength of premises in the statement and the method by which the conclusion is drawn. In formal logic, these are said to possess "material" and "formal" validity. Both the information (material) and the "form" of the argument must be correct or else the conclusion drawn from them will prove false.

Let us take a look at a premise as an example of this truism: "All men are mortal." Since we accept that as universal, when we recognize that "Robert E. Lee was a man," we conclude that "Robert E. Lee was mortal." Such a conclusion is clearly implied in the two premises and is, therefore, a valid conclusion. Had the original statement been "Some men are tall," "Robert E. Lee was a man," we could only conclude that Robert E. Lee *might* have been tall but could not be sure. Since this premise implies less, the conclusion, therefore, is not as certain and could never be described as "necessary."

We use inference many times a day. If, for example, I know the length of one side of an equilateral triangle, I can reason to the length of the other two. Again, one might think, "If this product is sold at Wal-mart, it will be good and be inexpensive." This product is sold there. Therefore it will be good and inexpensive. Or one might say "Whatever Gerald says cannot be trusted. This is what Gerald said about such and such. Therefore it cannot be trusted." Doctors use inference to diagnose patients, baseball managers use inference to plan their strategy, engineers use inference to design a bridge. Even the gift of flowers from a boy to a girl has a built in implication from which the giver hopes the receiver will draw an inference. The force of inference in the lives of all men and women is well established. It is an important part of how we think and reason.

A "necessary" inference, however, is one where the implication in the premises is so strong that the conclusion is considered absolutely certain. For example, "Only American-born persons may become president of the United States." Tony Blair is not American-born. Therefore, Tony Blair may not become president of the United States. Since the premises are certain, this conclusion is also certain. Again, someone might propose that "Only those who have held previous political office can be elected president." Robert Smith has not held previous political office. Therefore, Robert Smith cannot become president. While there is strong evidence to suggest that a previous political office is certainly the common way of rising to the presidency in the USA, this statement does not have the same certainty as the first one. It is not the law of the land and the Constitution did not require this, so it might be proven false at some future date. It is not therefore a *necessary* inference.

To give another case, this time biblical, in Romans 10:13-14 Paul gives a long series of inferences. Starting with Joel 2:32, which says "Whosoever shall call on the name of the Lord shall be saved" (ASV), Paul says we infer that before one could "call," he must first "believe;" and before such belief could exist in the mind of a man we infer that there must have been some "preaching," and from the fact that one has preached, we may infer that there must have been someone doing the "sending." Thus, what is implied, we may infer. Let me repeat that for emphasis: *What is implied by the text of Scripture may be inferred from the Scripture. The power does not lie in our inference from the text but in the implication of the text, that is to say, what is implied by the text.* God speaks through the text, so God is implying what the text implies.

Again Paul uses inference when he interprets Scripture in I Corinthians 15:27. Here he quotes Psalm 8:6: "He put all things in subjection under his feet" (ASV). He comments, however, that "it is evident that he is excepted who did subject all things unto him." The word "evident" indicates an implication from which we are to infer. So, he says, we infer that God, the one doing the subjecting, is excluded when he subjected everything else to Christ. This inference is not only logical, it is *necessary* owing to the omniscient nature of deity.

In Ephesians 4:8-10, Paul again employs an inference. Psalm 68:18 says "He ascended." But, says Paul, one may infer in the nature of the case that if one has ascended, he must first have been lower. There was first, then, he says, a descending. His reasoning is like this: All who ascend are included in those who have first been lower. Christ ascended. Therefore Christ must first have been lower. This inference is not only logical, it is also *necessary* owing to the very nature of things. It is imminently rational, and denying it would be irrational.

Not only do Bible writers use inference in interpreting other scriptures they also often use inference in their discussion and expect us to follow it. Paul uses the form of a hypothetical syllogism in I Corinthians 15:17 when he says "If [and only if] Christ be not raised, then your faith is vain" (KJV). He expects the reader mentally to add, "My faith is not vain, and, therefore, Christ is raised." The logic of his conclusion is irrefutable. And, make no mistake about it, this is rational thought at its best.

Hebrews 7:7 gives another instance of a Bible writer's using inference and expecting us to follow it with a rational approach to his statement. "But without any dispute the less is blessed of the better" (ASV). Based on that, the writer expects us to accept that Melchizedek is greater than Abraham. In verse 12, he adds another: "For the priesthood being changed, there is made of necessity a change also of the law." In paraphrase, he says, if the priesthood is changed, it is a necessary inference that the law with which it is associated is changed. In a more precise statement, his argument is this: All laws whose priesthood is changed must be changed in other respects too. The priesthood of the Law of Moses was changed. Therefore, the Law of Moses must be changed in other respects too. If it is assumed that the Law of Moses is still in effect precisely as it was before the cross, none of this could possibly be true. The logic would be faulty. But the logic is not faulty, it is rock-solid.

In yet another case, Paul certainly encouraged the Corinthians to use some "common sense" logic in understanding his statement "not to have company with fornicators." In I Corinthians 5:9-11, he told them they should have known that he was referring to fornicators in the church and not outside. But how could they have come to such a conclusion? He had intended for them to reason along these lines: If I am to avoid all contact with fornicators outside the church, I must isolate myself from society. I cannot isolate myself from society (because I must seek to convert them to Christ and must be as salt and light to them). So I cannot avoid all fornicators outside the church. The conclusion that they drew from this was unavoidable because it was logically necessary.

Nowhere in scripture are we told specifically that the Sabbath provision has been taken away. When we read, however, that Christ has "blotted out the bond written in ordinances" (Col. 2:14, ASV), we understand that the Sabbath provision would have to be included in what is blotted out. And, Paul goes on to note that the Sabbath must not be used to judge Christians in their faithfulness to God (2:16). This is a logical progression also, which builds upon the implications of the statement in 2:14. In another case, the Bible teaches that elders are to be the husband of one wife (1 Tim. 3:2). From this we infer that only men can be elders because only men can be husbands. We could go on and on with this, but the message is plain. If we care what God has had to say in Scripture we must attempt to draw correct conclusions from rock-solid foundational premises.

Some say we should not use this method for establishing authority because it is based on human logic. This ought not to deter us though. In point of fact, even following commands requires the use of the mind to understand language and the use of examples is based on the mental ability of establishing a precedent from cases (a form of reasoning by generalization). So to eliminate basic functions of the mind for reasoning and for language would leave us with no ability to use Scripture. As we have previously noted, reasoning is an essential part of the mental capability God gave us and, as seen in many instances in the Scripture itself, he clearly intends that we should use it wisely and well in understanding his Word.

Conclusion

The religion of our day has become largely a "lazy man's religion." It seeks for easy ways out, and seldom accepts the real challenge of being Christian. Christianity comes with a built-in work ethic. Most folks today are not interested in this, since easier ways that require little thought and almost no action are so readily available. Therefore, they have accepted a counterfeit version of Christianity that allows them to barely think at all and make no real demands of them. Subjectivism and its high-sounding counterpart existentialism are extremely popular, even though they are so in very subtle and almost unidentifiable ways. Most who are held in the grip of their devastating talons would never admit to it any more than they would confess to the spiritual laziness that empowers these philosophies in the first place. Paul's caution to us should be sufficient to warn us away from these dangerous ways of thinking and acting: "See to it that no one takes you captive by philosophy and empty deceit, according to human tradition, according to the elemental spirits of the world, and not according to Christ" (Col. 2:8, ESV).

Selected Bibliography

Campbell, Alexander. *The Christian System*. Cincinnati: Bosworth, Chase & Hall, Publishers, 1871.

King, Dan, and Boyd, Leon. *Responsibility and Authority in the Spiritual Realm*. Bowling Green, KY: GOTF, 1992.

King, D. H. "Paul and the Tannaim: A study in Galatians," *WTJ* 45 (1983), 340-70

Lockhart, Clinton. *Principles of Interpretation*. Revised edition. Delight, AR: Gospel Light Publishing Co., 1915.

Machen, J. Gresham. *Christianity and Liberalism*. Grand Rapids: Eerdmans,1923.

McAllister, L. A., and Tucker, W. A. *Journey in Faith: A History of the Christian Church (Disciples of Christ)*. St. Louis: Bethany Press, 1975.

Music, Goebel. *Behold the Pattern*. Colleyville, TX: Goebel Music Publications, 1991.

North, Stafford. "Command, Example and Necessary Inference." http://faculty.oc.edu/stafford.north/comm-ex-inf.htm

Thomas, J. D. *Heaven's Window*. Abilene, TX: Biblical Research Press, 1974.

Waddey, John. "*Voices of Concern* Were Voices of Change." http://www.christianity-then-and-now.com/html/review_016.html

3

CHURCH SUPPORT
OF HUMAN INSTITUTIONS

PAUL EARNHART

Controversy over the relationship of churches to human
institutions has a long history among churches of Christ in the
United States but it reached a climax during the late 1950's
and the early 1960's. It was a very turbulent time and all those
who lived through it can testify to that fact. In the mid 1950's
in the pages of the Gospel Advocate an essential quarantine
was called for all gospel preachers who objected to human
institutions being funded by churches. I was preaching in
Kenosha, Wisconsin, partially supported by a church which
was the sponsor of a national radio and television program
called The Herald of Truth. In 1955 I attended a debate in
Abilene Texas in which two men, Earnest R. Harper and Yater
Tant, debated the question of one church sponsoring a work
they were unable to finance alone by soliciting contributions
from other churches. Two debates had already been held

between Guy N. Woods and Roy Cogdill on churches support of orphan homes.

During this time scheduled gospel meetings with men opposed to the above arrangements were canceled, churches were divided, preachers were let go. Families were divided in sentiment. Long time friends were separated. Old comrades parted company. It was not just a challenging time intellectually (the need to study the controverted issues through thoroughly) but emotionally.

As is often true in controversy, people align themselves for reasons other than the scripture and are so intent on proving the other fellow wrong that they do not listen very well to what he has to say. It is therefore most likely that many during that time hardly knew what the issue was. For some it became a matter of who was on which side or how someone who represented a certain viewpoint behaved himself, or in many cases people were swayed by popular but often unsubstantiated stories that made the rounds.

The Controversy Developed Gradually

The controversy over support by local churches of human organizations did not begin suddenly. It had been a matter for discussion among brethren long before it became a divisive issue. A. B. Barrett, the founder of Abilene Christian College (now University) wrote the following in the March 13, 1930 issue of the *Gospel Advocate*:

> There were no 'brotherhood colleges,' church orphanages,' 'old folks homes,' and the like, among apostolic congregations.... Individual Christians, any number, may scripturally engage in any worthwhile work, such as running colleges, papers, and orphanages, and other individual Christians may properly assist them in every proper way; but no local congregations should be called upon as such, to contribute a thing to any such enterprise. Such a call would be out of harmony with the word of the living God. And if any congregation so contributes, it transcends its scriptural

prerogatives.

W. E. Brightwell wrote prophetically in the November 29, 1934 issue of the same magazine: "Institutionalism has destroyed the life and energy of the church today!.. .... The next religious war will be fought around the issue of institutionalism." Guy N. Woods said in the Abilene Christian College lectures of 1939: "The ship of Zion has foundered more than once on the sandbar of institutionalism. The tendency to organize is a characteristic of the age. On the theory that the end justifies the means, brethren have now scrupled to form organizations in the church to do the work the church itself was designed to do. All such organizations usurp the work of the church, and are unnecessary and sinful." Again in the December 15, 1946 issue of the *Annual Lesson Commentary* he wrote: "There is no place for charitable organizations in the work of the New Testament church. It is the only charitable organization that the Lord authorizes, or that is needed to do the work the Lord expects his people to do." But things changed dramatically when the multiplication of such institutions after World War II brought the issue to prominence. Many aspects of this question developed amidst the controversy and were shaped by it. The institutions themselves by their very number and increasing stake in the question added to the resistance to any opposition. The truth is that by the time the opposition to this practice solidified these ancillary organizations were already so entrenched in the treasuries of the churches that it was too late to stem the tide of support for them among the majority of brethren.

Un-Christlike Behavior and Carnal Motives

An unfortunate but real aspect of such controversies among Christians is that the shallow influence of the gospel on the character of many is exposed. Passionate feelings on both sides at times erupted in such a carnal way that it belied any sense of brotherhood. All this likely made it difficult for those earnest souls who were trying to decide the issue by which side the "good people" were on. Misbehavior on both sides of the dispute made this impossible. There were good people on both sides as well as some who in the fever of conflict forgot how Christians ought to behave. There were some cases of physical combat and even more cases of intemperate verbal attacks. It was a very sad time. For those that were wise the issue had to be decided by avoiding the party spirit entirely and determining the question in the light of God's word -- regardless of consequences. That is not to say that all the brethren dealt with the issue in that way. Some simply took the course of least resistance and were influenced by family ties, certain preachers or gospel papers, or their emotions. Some no doubt acquiesced out of an aversion to controversy or simple indifference.

Fortunately in the midst of this very emotional turmoil some wrote and spoke with courtesy and brotherly affection and addressed the issue biblically rather than with personal attacks. This focused the question at hand on God's will rather than on the character of the disputants (e.g. the Arlington Meeting). A good man is not right in his position because he is good nor a bad man wrong in his position because he is bad. Truth is vindicated by the scriptures although an unworthy witness to it certainly does not "adorned the doctrine of God" (Titus 2:10, NKJV). It must also be stated that many who defended the churches support of human institutions were driven by selfless motives and concern for the good work they were doing. But, of course, the issue was not about whether they were doing good work, but (1) whether the good work they were doing was a work God had given the churches and (2) if it was a work given by the Lord to the churches shouldn't they be doing it rather than handing it over to human institutions who were seeking financial support from the churches.

Amidst the good motives driving the building of human institutions to do the work of the churches there was a spirit not so noble. That was the rising force of "denominational" pride which, fed by the growing prosperity of brethren and churches, took great delight in these institutions, as well as the construction of fine new meeting houses, and the higher educational background of the preachers. We were not to be any longer a backwater religious curiosity but a force to be reckoned with. Now we had our own benevolent institutions and our own national radio and television programs and a far more aggressive work of foreign evangelism like the churches among the denominations. Rather than rejoicing in the greatness of God and His Son and the truth of the gospel we began to delight in our growing standing in the culture. It was a subtle but real seduction. It remains a continuing challenge for God's people. The Old Testament church was seduced by a desire to be like the nations in their carnal glory and idolatrous worship (1 Sam. 8:1-8) . God's New Testament people have been and still can be drawn away by the same pathetic emptiness. In serving Christ we are not to ape the world (1 cor. 3:19) or seek to please men (Gal. 1:10) or seek glory for ourselves but to please God always (1 John 3:22) and glorify Him in all things (1 Pet. 4:11).

Some Issues that Arose Amidst the Controversy

At the beginning of the dispute over institutionalism there was disagreement among those who defended church support of benevolent organizations as to how they were to be set up. Generally, brethren east of the Mississippi argued that they had to be controlled by private boards because it was not scriptural for the churches to be over and direct a "home". Most often brethren west of the Mississippi believed that orphan care institutions under a board were not scriptural and should be under the eldership of a local church (Boles Home in Quinlan, Texas was widely opposed because it was under a board). The latter approach usually involved a "sponsoring church" arrangement with other churches sending funds to the church "sponsoring" the care facility. Over time as opposition to both approaches grew this disagreement was largely laid aside as the defenders joined league to make a united response.

Another issue that was not present at the beginning of the controversy (not our subject but raised by it) was the question of whether churches were scripturally authorized to engage in general benevolence, i.e. to provide for the needs of non-Christians. It was generally presumed as the dispute arose that it was permissible for local churches to provide for orphans but not through some institution other than the local church. In the course of the controversy, however, some began to ask if there was any biblical evidence that churches sent to the relief of non-Christians and concluded that all the evidence pointed to the relief of "saints" (Acts 2:44-45; 4:34-37; 6:1-3; 11:27-30; Rom. 15:25-28; 1 Cor. 16:1-4; 2 Cor. 9:12-13). The issue was never whether orphans (and widows) among the unsaved should be cared for but whether that was a task given to the churches or to individual Christians. Those who defended general benevolence appealed either to passages which were addressed to the individual Christian (Gal. 6:10; James 1:27) or to a passage in 2 Corinthians 9:13. Of Galatians 6:10 it was argued that the letter was addressed to "the churches of Galatia" (Gal. 1:2) and therefore all in the letter must be intended to authorize church action. This can hardly be true unless all the instruction in letters addressed to churches authorizes the collective function of the church regardless of context. Some of the exhortations in the epistles are clearly addressed to individuals -- to husbands, to wives, to children, to masters and to servants (Eph. 5:22-6:9 and Col. 3:18-4:1). And the instructions to "labor" and "work" in Ephesians. 5:28 and 1 Thessalonians. 3:10, certainly addressed to individuals, would put congregations into business and labor for a living if applied to the churches. The contexts of both Galatians 6:10 and James 1:27 show them to be spoken to individuals. As for 2 Corinthians 9:13 Paul is speaking of the collection for the saints in Jerusalem (v. 12) and the fact that the generosity of the Gentile churches would move their Jewish brethren to glorify God in thanksgiving "for your liberal sharing with them, and <u>with all.</u>" The distinction here is not Christians and non-Christians but Christians in Jerusalem and all (other Christians). There is simply no clear evidence to the contrary.

The Institutional Question

But let us now presume that we are speaking of support by local churches of other institutions which are engaged in work clearly given to local churches to do. Is there any evidence that the apostolic churches gave any of their God ordained work into the hands of human organizations who were then financially supported by them? I think most all would agree that there is no biblical evidence of such. In the absence of such evidence those who support such a practice have argued that these organizations are just expedient methods of doing the work assigned to the churches, i.e. song books (unmentioned in Scripture), church buildings (unmentioned in scripture). This was the approach of J. D. Thomas in his book *We Be Brethren*[1] and in his addresses in the *Arlington Meeting*.[2] Of course to make this argument he uses a passage (James 1:27) that is not given to the churches. The problem with the argument itself is that it is not just a method used by the church and overseen and guided by the church to do its work. It is a totally

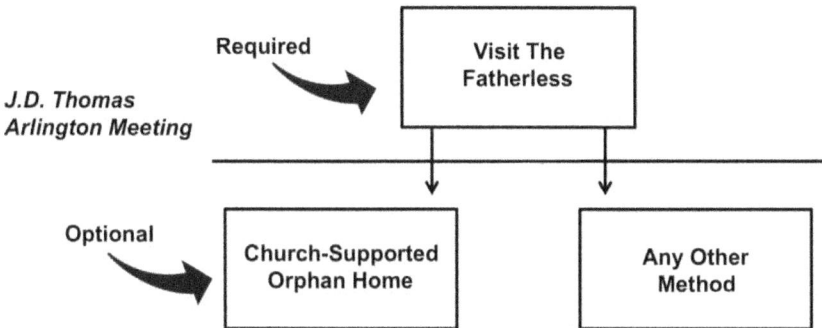

separate institution to which the church surrenders both the work and its oversight and becomes merely the source of donated funds. It is not the same as the church buying goods to feed needy saints or buying medical services to treat them. These would be methods the church uses to do its work. The same kind of reasoning used to justify a church supported child care institution as a means of meeting its benevolent responsibility could also be used to justify a church supported college to meet its edification responsibilities and a church

---

1 J. D. Thomas, *We Be Brethren: A Study in Biblical Interpretation* (Abilene, TX: Biblical Research Press, 1958).

2 J. D. Thomas. "J. D. Thomas" In *The Arlington Meeting*, comp. Cecil Willis. Marion, Indiana: Cogdill Foundation, 1976.

supported missionary society to meet its evangelistic obligations. In both these latter cases both the work and oversight of the work is yielded to another institution. And that is exactly what happened. This argument came to be used to justify church support of colleges, and to obtain that support (Lipscomb University et. al.); and to justify church support of evangelistic organizations and to obtain that support (World Bible School et. al.). In the New Testament the churches themselves did the work assigned to them and were fully equipped to do so. That is obvious in the care of the poor in the young church in Jerusalem (Acts 2:44-45; 4:34-37) and later in the case of the poor widows (Acts 6:1-3). There is also no indication that Paul's instruction to Timothy about the church's responsibility to care for Christian "widows who are really widows" (1 Tim. 5:3-10) was accomplished by turning over the work and its oversight to another organization and then sending them a regular donation. In all these cases the so-called "expedient" violates the New Testament pattern of church order and function and is not an expedient but an unscriptural addition.

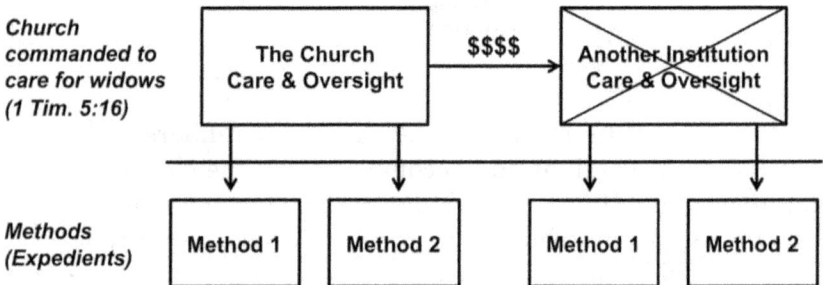

Church commanded to care for widows (1 Tim. 5:16)	The Church Care & Oversight	$$$$ →	Another Institution Care & Oversight (crossed out)
Methods (Expedients)	Method 1 / Method 2		Method 1 / Method 2

Brother J. D. Thomas made the same argument to justify the "sponsoring church" arrangement. The problem with this approach is that the "sponsoring church" is not just another method, an optional expedient used by churches to do their work. It actually creates another organization out of a local church and makes use of its elders for purposes they were never divinely ordained to fulfill, i.e. to oversee the work of other churches in the field of benevolence, evangelism or edification (Acts 14:23; 20:28; 1 Pet. 5:1,2.).

The Church Support of Colleges

As has been already noted the churches support of child care organizations, especially those under an independent board, was used as a springboard to justify the support of "Christian" colleges. If it is scriptural for the churches to support separate institutions to meet their benevolent obligations, the argument went, it must also be scriptural for the churches to support organizations to meet their edification responsibilities since the colleges are training their preachers and other workers. Moreover it was important for these colleges to get their support from the churches so that they might be kept biblically sound. Well known preacher, N. B. Hardeman, one of the founders of Freed Hardeman College (now university), was one of the early proponents of this practice although G. C. Brewer, another well known preacher, had raised the matter even earlier. In the October 23, 1947 issue of the *Gospel Advocate* brother Hardeman wrote:

> I have always believed that a church has the right to contribute to a school or an orphanage if it so desired. In all that I have written there is no conflict on this matter. The right to contribute to one is the right to contribute to the other. Note the parallel: (1) The school is a human institution; it has a board of directors: it teaches secular branches in connection with the Bible. (2) An orphan home is a human institution; it has a board of directors; it teaches secular branches in connection with the Bible. The same principle that permits one must also permit the other. They must stand or fall together. Assuming that the school does the work of the church (which is subject to discussion) then may I ask; if the church can do part of its work -- caring for orphans -- through a human institution, why can it not do another part of its work -- teaching the Bible -- through a human institution? These brethren failed to show *why*. According to the 'ace writer' the church sins in contributing to either. . . . Why will these brethren support an orphanage and fight the schools? The possible answer is that there are too many of our best

churches that support the orphan home, and these brethren are afraid to attack them.[3]

In 1963 Batsell Barrett Baxter, preacher for the Hillsboro church in Nashville and head of the Bible Department at David Lipscomb College presented three lessons to the church affirming the churches right and responsibility to support the colleges. These lessons were published in a booklet in which brother Baxter echoed brother Hardeman: "Some who are agreed that the church can contribute to an orphan's home are not convinced that the church can contribute to a Christian school. It is difficult to see a significant difference so far as principle is concerned. The orphan's home and the Christian school must stand or fall together."[4] He went further: "The fact that the church must provide preachers, elders, teachers, and wives of such leaders places the responsibility for training and nurturing the young upon the church. Both of God's institutions have the responsibility to participate in this training program."[5] He went on to say: "If Christian schools are needed and can be used by the church to train its young, does this not establish a strong implication that the church might have some responsibility in starting such schools and causing them to be available when young people have need for them? If schools are needed to train leaders for the church, does this not imply that the church needs to help get the schools ready to provide such training?"[6] And then he concludes: "Actually, the church has depended upon these schools for many years to play a major role in training of preachers, elders, teachers, and others. Is it not right that the church should provide the funds for the training of its own leaders?"[7] In addition he warns:

If the churches do not support the schools, ultimately

---

3 844.

4 Batsell Barrett Baxter, *Questions and Issues of the Day* (Nashville, TN: Hillsboro Church of Christ, 1964), 39.

5 Ibid., 26.

6 Ibid., 26-27.

7 Ibid., 29.

one of two alternatives will result. One real possibility is that the schools will die . . . . . If the church does not support Christian schools, the second alternative is that the schools will eventually turn elsewhere for their support. When they turn to business and industry for any significant portion of their regular support it becomes inevitable that the Christian purposes for which the schools were established will be forgotten . . . . . .It is my conviction that the schools need to be dependent upon the churches for the financial life blood in order for the schools to remain permanently loyal to the goals and principles which the Bible teaches."[8]

You can see the line of argumentation. It is presumed by brother Baxter that the churches need the schools to survive and to meet their responsibility to train workers in the churches. It is amazing that an institution so necessary to the work of the churches does not appear anywhere in the New Testament. For our brother the schools are not a mere expedient but a necessity. His argument from the orphan home, like that of brother Hardeman, is based on the presumption that no one will question the scripturalness of the church support of orphan homes and are therefore bound not to object to the churches support of schools. This kind of argument from established present practice may be logical but proves nothing biblically. A proposed practice is not proven to be from God by its similarity to what is already being done. All must be grounded in the clear teaching of the New Testament. Otherwise we will be found moving from one unscriptural arrangement to the next and from that one to another, all equally unknown in God's word. In this very way Christians have been led from precedent to precedent until they are removed very far away from the will of heaven. We are not opposed to the care of indigent children. How could anyone with an ounce of compassion be. But it rests with individual disciples to respond to such need as they have opportunity and ability. We are not opposed to colleges operated by Christians but theirs is not a function of local churches but of the home

---

8 Ibid., 29-30.

and individual Christians.

It did not take long for brother Reuel Lemmons, editor of the Firm Foundation, to respond in print to brother Baxter's booklet. He did so with regret, he wrote, because of his close friendship with and high regard for the author but he felt the issue was not a matter of indifference but of faith. Lemmons objected on two grounds. First, it was his conviction that the work God had given to the churches should be done by the churches and be under the oversight of the elders of those churches. And though he had supported the care of needy children under the oversight of local church elders and the sponsoring church arrangement to fund such work, he objected strenuously on biblical grounds to churches supporting separate organizations under a board and therefore rejected Baxter's analogy of orphan homes and colleges. Secondly, he rejected the work of the colleges as being the work of the churches. Lemmons was mistaken, we believe, in his view that God had called the churches to general benevolence and in his support of the sponsoring church arrangement but correct in his objection to the churches doing their work through a separate organization, and especially one which was not doing work assigned to the churches in the first place. In his own words: "A board is not the church. Therefore a board cannot fulfill 1 Timothy 5:16. Only the church (corporate body) can do that. The charge is given to an autonomous church but not to an autonomous board. If the church is charged in 1 Timothy 5:16 with doing a work, the very charge excludes the passing of the buck to something which is not the church."[9] As to the genesis of this controversy Lemmons wrote: "It has been my contention from the beginning that brethren are not so much interested in church support of homes under boards, but they are interested in contending for that in order to ease into a campaign for church support of colleges."[10]

This conflict over how the churches should accomplish their

---

9 As reprinted in *Truth Magazine*, June 1964, from the *Firm Foundation*.

10 Ibid.

child care work was significant for a while but as earlier noted in time was pushed to the background in the face of opposition to both arrangements.

"Missionary Society" Arrangements for Evangelism

As could have been predicted the argument that separate institutions as mere expedients for churches to do their work in benevolence would be used to justify the churches use of separate organizations to do their appointed work in other areas. This has happened in the field of evangelism. One such organization is World Bible School which was founded by Jimmy Lovell in 1971 as a non-profit organization to teach the lost worldwide by the use of Bible correspondence courses. It is supported by the regular contribution of churches and individuals. When Lovell died in 1984 it is somewhat ironic that Reuel Lemmons who had objected so strenuously 20 years before to churches doing their work through human organizations became director of the WBS organization and editor of its new journal, *Action*. It was Lemmons himself who exploded the effort by some to distinguish these human arrangements from the missionary society by arguing that the thing that was wrong with the missionary society was its control of the churches and not the fact that the churches were doing their evangelistic work through it. He wrote: "I have seen various attempts to tell what is wrong with the missionary society. The society is not wrong simply because it dominates the churches; that could be corrected. It is wrong because it is a gospel preaching arrangement set up under a board, to do the work God gave the church to do which supplants the church in this area. It is an organization other than the church, not controlled by the elders whom God ordained to have the oversight of the work of the church.

WBS is currently headquartered in Austin, Texas. In explaining the nature of the organization which he founded brother Lovell wrote in 1983: "Legally, and again I have never been questioned, we are incorporated under the laws of California as West Coast Christian Publishing Co. -- a non-profit, tax deductible religious organization. We have another corporation in Texas known as World Bible School, with directors who are on the WCC board. In neither organization have we ever had any conflict of purpose."[11] In 1986 a writer in *Action* explained the nature of the organization as follow: "WBS is an organization that employs a method of teaching, provides the contact between students and teacher, employs workers to do 'follow-up' work on the student and solicits contributions from churches for its work. We would like to see more churches financially supporting WBS. Small churches that do no mission work because they are small would find themselves responsible for more baptisms than more large churches if they simply sent a monthly check to WBS to help with this good work. Mention it to the leaders and elders where you worship and ask that they consider doing it."[12]

WBS currently claims to be teaching 2 million students around the world and credits their work with many baptisms and the formation of many churches. We have no quarrel with their aim of teaching the gospel in the world. It should be the passion of every church and every disciple of Jesus Christ. But we do object to any humanly arranged organization that proposes to do the work of the churches for them and solicits money from them to that end. In that they differ not at all in principle from the missionary societies of the 19th and 20th centuries. Whether intended or not the upshot of creating such human institutions to do the work assigned to the churches is to call into question the wisdom of the Almighty. Are we to be wiser than God? Can we not trust His arrangements to accomplish His purposes? Without missionary organizations of any sort save the churches the early Christians sent the gospel around the world before the first century closed (Col. 1:6, 23).

How are We to Avoid this Rejection of Divine Wisdom in the Future?

First, by a deep reverence for the perfect and infinite wisdom of God. As Paul wrote to the Romans: "Oh the depth of the riches

---

11 *Action*, Sept., 1983, 2.

12 Ibid., March, 1986, 2.

both of the wisdom and knowledge of God! How unsearchable are His judgments and His ways past finding out! For who has known the mind of the Lord? Or who has become His counselor? Or who has first given to Him and it shall be repaid to him? For of Him and through Him and to Him are all things, to whom be glory forever. Amen." (Rom. 11:33-36). Creatures cannot become the instructors of the Creator. The attempt to do so would be preposterous on our part and most arrogant. To truly know God is to know ourselves and our human limitations. We cannot anticipate His infinite mind because He does not think as we think (Isa. 55:6-9). Out task is to listen, to learn and to obey (1 Sam. 3:9).

Second, by the disposition to always consult the will of God before taking any action in His name. This will save us from the folly of first looking around to see what men in their wisdom are thinking and doing that is apparently "succeeding," and imitating it. God's purposes for us can only be only accomplished by following His ways. The wisdom of this world is foolishness with God (1 Cor. 1:20) and it ought to be foolishness to His children. To turn from God's way to our own is "iniquity" (Isa. 53:6). If we truly trust God and love Him His word will be the last word for us.

4

SCOPE OF CHURCH BENEVOLENCE

CARROL SUTTON

The subject assigned to me is: "Church Benevolence – Limited or Unlimited?" This is a subject (like many others) over which there are different views among brethren. The truth as revealed in the New Testament is important and very valuable. John 1:17 says, "For the law was given by Moses, but grace and truth came by Jesus Christ" (KJV[1]). Jesus said in John 8:32, "And ye shall know the truth, and the truth shall make you free." In praying to the Father in John 17:17 Jesus said, "Sanctify them through thy truth: thy word is truth." Speaking to the apostles in John 14:26 Jesus said that "...he (the Holy Ghost – C.S.) shall teach you all things, and bring all things to your remembrance, whatsoever I have said unto you." He also said to them in John 16:13: "Howbeit when he the Spirit of truth is come, he will guide you into all truth..." The truth, the

---

1 Unless otherwise noted, all Scripture quotations taken from KJV.

faith, the law of liberty, the gospel is the word of God by which we will be judged. According to Galatians 2:11-14 we are to walk "uprightly according to the truth of the gospel!" We are here to study the New Testament to learn what the truth is on this subject.

Let us briefly define the key terms of our subject: "Church Benevolence - Limited or Unlimited?"

By "church" I mean a local congregation of saints acting in a congregational capacity, that is, as a body, as a collectivity, as a church, under the direction of its elders, and by means of the church treasury. I do not mean individuals acting in their individual capacities as they may decide to do so by means of their own resources.

By "benevolence" I mean the giving of assistance, help or aid such as food, clothing, shelter and medical care for the relief of the physical needs of others.

A side note is that the English word "benevolence" appears only one time in the King James Version of the New Testament. It is in 1 Corinthians 7:3 where it says: "Let the husband render unto the wife due benevolence..." The New King James Version says: "Let the husband render to his wife the affection due her..." The word that is translated "benevolence" appears only one other time in the King James Version. It is found in Ephesians 6:7 where it is translated "good will". In neither case does it refer to the relief of others as we are discussing in this lesson.

"Benevolence" is defined by Webster to mean: "1: disposition to do good 2 a : an act of kindness b: a generous gift..."[2] As we relieve others, we are being benevolent to them.

By "limited" I mean "confined within limits: RESTRICTED." It is only for those for whom the church, in its congregational capacity, is authorized to relieve. They are widows indeed (1 Tim. 5:16) and certain other needy ones among those who are

---

2 *Webster's NSCD*

called believers (Acts 2:44-45; Acts 4:32-35), disciples (Acts 6:1-7), brethren (Acts 11:27-30), saints (1 Cor. 16:1-2; Rom. 15:25-31; 2 Cor. 8 and 9).

By "unlimited" I mean *not* "confined within limits;" *not* "restricted"! I mean *no* boundary, but open to all! This would allow the church, acting in its congregational capacity, to extend its benevolence (physical relief) to any or to all! This would include alien sinners of all kinds regardless of their condition or situation. Personally, I know of no one who really believes that church benevolence is unlimited although many will assert that it is!

Who Are the Subjects of Church Benevolence?

To learn for whom the church, as such, is to relieve, our appeal must be to the Scriptures. Let us consider the following Scriptures.

Acts 2:44-45
"And all that *believed* were together, and had all things common; And sold their possessions and goods, and parted (NKJV – 'divided') them to all men, as every man had need." Note: This may or may not be "church benevolence", but it is a case of saints helping believers!

Acts 4:32, 34-35
"And the multitude of them that *believed* were of one heart and of one soul: neither said any of them that ought of the things which he possessed was his own; but they had all things common...Neither was there any *among them* that lacked: for as many as were possessors of lands or houses sold them, and brought the prices of the things that were sold, And laid them down at the apostles' feet: and distribution was made unto every man according as he had need." Note: Here we have a church acting in its congregational capacity, relieving the physical needs of those who were *believers*!

Acts 6:1-6
From this passage we learn that "...when the number of the *disciples* was multiplied", the Grecian widows "were neglected

in the daily ministration." There were seven men chosen by the congregation and appointed by the apostles over the business of serving tables. Note: This was a local church acting in its congregational capacity relieving the needs of *disciples*!

Acts 11:29-30
"Then the *disciples*, every man according to his ability, determined to send relief unto the *brethren* which dwelt in Judea: Which also they did, and *sent to the elders* by the hands of Barnabas and Saul." Note: The disciples in Antioch, acting as a unit, a collective, a congregation, sent relief to the *brethren* which dwelt in Judea. They sent it *to the elders* by the hands of Barnabas and Saul.

1 Corinthians 16:1-3
"Now concerning the collection *for the saints*, as I have given order to the churches of Galatia, even so do ye. Upon the first day of the week let every one of you lay by him in store, as God hath prospered him, that there be no gatherings when I come. And when I come, whomsoever ye shall approve by your letters, them will I send to bring your liberality unto Jerusalem." Note: The church at Corinth was given an order "concerning the collection *for the saints*". That same order had been given to the churches of Galatia. This collection, this contribution, this liberality, this bounty, this gift was for poor *saints* in Jerusalem.

2 Corinthians 8
Paul tells the church at Corinth about "the grace of God bestowed on the churches of Macedonia" (v. 1) . Although they were in deep poverty, they were liberal in giving to help the poor *saints* in Jerusalem. In verses 3 & 4 he said, "For to their power, I bear record, yea, and beyond their power they were willing of themselves; Praying us with much entreaty that we would receive the gift, and take upon us the fellowship of the *ministering to the saints*." In verse 7b Paul said, "...see that ye abound in this grace also." This was the grace of giving. In verse 11 he further said, "Now therefore perform the doing of it; that as there was a readiness to will, so there may a performance also out of that which ye have." In verses 16-23

Paul mentioned that Titus and others were "messengers of the churches", chosen of the churches, to travel with Paul to administer this contribution or gift to those poor *saints* in Jerusalem

Romans 15:25-32

"But now I go unto Jerusalem to minister unto the saints. For it hath pleased them of Macedonia and Achaia to make a certain contribution *for the poor saints* which are at Jerusalem. It hath pleased them verily; and their debtors they are. For if the Gentiles have been made partakers of their spiritual things, their duty is also to minister unto them in carnal things (NKJV-'material things'). When therefore I have performed this, and have sealed to them this fruit, I will come by you into Spain. And I am sure that, when I come unto you, I shall come in the fulness of the blessing of the gospel of Christ. Now I beseech you, brethren, for the Lord Jesus Christ's sake, and for the love of the Spirit, that ye strive together with me in your prayers to God for me; That I may be delivered from them that do not believe in Judea; and that my service which I have for Jerusalem may be accepted *of the saints*; That I may come unto you with joy by the will of God, and may with you be refreshed." Verse 25 says "...I go unto Jerusalem to minister unto the *saints!*" Verse 26 says "For it hath pleased them of Macedonia and Achaia to make a certain contribution for the poor *saints* which are at Jerusalem!" In verses 30-32 Paul begged the Christians in Rome to pray for him that he would "be delivered from" *those who did not believe* in Judea and that the service (help) that he had for Jerusalem would "be accepted of the *saints*." Question: Did Paul desire to be delivered from those he was going to help? Obviously not! His service was *not* for the poor sinners but *for the poor saints!*

2 Corinthians 9:1-13

"For as touching the ministering to the *saints*, it is superfluous for me to write to you..." (v. 1). In verses 12-14 we read: "For the administration of this service not only supplieth the want of the *saints*, but is abundant also by many thanksgivings unto God; Whiles by the experiment of this ministration they glorify God for your professed subjection unto the gospel of Christ, and *for your liberal distribution unto them, and unto all men*; And by their prayer for you, which long after you for the exceeding grace of God in you." Let us make some observations about the expression: "...for your liberal distribution unto them and unto all *men*" in verse 13.

In the expression, "for your liberal distribution unto them and unto all *men*", "*men*" is in italics in the King James Version which indicates that it is not in the Greek text. The American Standard Version says "unto them and unto all". Young's Literal Translation and the NASB say "to them and to all".

Are there any limitations on the expression "to them and to all?" It is obvious that the pronoun "them" of verse 13 has "saints" of verse 12 as its antecedent. In I Corinthians 16:1-3 in writing to the church at Corinth Paul had said: "...them (speaking of men the church would approve – C.S.) will I send to bring your liberality unto Jerusalem." We learn from Romans 15:26 that the contribution was "for the poor *saints*" or as stated in the American Standard Version "for the poor among the *saints*" at Jerusalem.

Let us keep in mind that the contribution was for "saints"! Was it for every saint everywhere or was it limited? It was "for the poor among the saints" at Jerusalem! It was limited!

What does the expression "and to all *men*" mean? Is it unlimited as some of our brethren contend? Many contend that it was for both saints and sinners! If it is not limited it would include "all sinners" everywhere! It would take a large, huge, an enormous contribution to accommodate all sinners everywhere! Can you imagine how much food, clothing, etc. it would take to care for "all sinners" everywhere at that time in the first century? If it means "all *men*" without any qualification, limitation or restriction, that would make the collection, the contribution, the gift too large! I don't think that any serious minded student of the Scriptures really believes that the expression "and to all *men*" is unlimited or without limitations. Do you? Surely not.

Let us consider some facts about the contribution, the

collection, the liberality, the service, the gift, that was a liberal distribution that was administered by Paul and "the messengers of the churches" that is said have been "unto them and unto all *men*" in 2 Corinthians 9:13. To *whom* does the expression "unto them and unto all *men* (or "all") refer since *men* is in italics and no part of the text?

(1) The funds which made up the gift, the contribution, the service, the bounty, were raised "*for the saints*". In 1 Corinthians 16:1 Paul says: "Now concerning the collection *for the saints*, as I have given order to the churches of Galatia, even so do ye." For whom were they to be used? The funds were to be used for those for whom they were raised! The *saints*!

(2) In Romans 15:25 Paul said: "But now I go unto Jerusalem to *minister unto the saints*." Question: Unto whom was Paul going to minister in Jerusalem? He was going to Jerusalem "to minister unto the saints".

(3) In Romans 15:26 Paul says: "For it hath pleased them of Macedonia and Achaia to make a certain contribution for the poor *saints* which are at Jerusalem." Question: For whom were those of Macedonia and Achaia pleased to make a certain contribution? They were pleased to make a contribution for the poor *saints* which were at Jerusalem!

(4) Speaking of the saints in Macedonia, in 2 Corinthians 8:4, Paul said: "Praying us with much entreaty that we would receive the gift, and take upon us the fellowship of the ministering to the saints." Question: The Macedonians implored Paul (and those with him) to receive the gift, and take upon them the "fellowship of the ministering" to whom? The answer is very plain and clear. The *saints*!

(5) In 2 Corinthians 9:1 Paul said: "For as touching the ministering to the *saints*, it is superfluous for me to write unto you." Question: To whom was the ministering that Paul mentions here? Paul said this "ministering" was "to the *saints*."

(6) Paul wrote to the saints at Rome in Romans 15:30-31 requesting them to pray for him. He said: "That I may be delivered from them that do not believe in Judea; and that my service which I have for Jerusalem may be accepted of the saints." Question: From whom did Paul desire to be delivered when he went "to Jerusalem to minister unto the *saints*"? Paul desired to be delivered from *sinners*? He said: "from them that do not believe in Judea"? Question: Who did Paul desire would accept the service (v. 25 – contribution) that he had for Jerusalem? Paul desired that his service would "be accepted of the *saints*"! Question: In view of the fact that Paul wanted *to be delivered from the sinners* in Judea and desired that his service would be accepted *of the saints*, is it unreasonable to think that Paul's service went *to the saints* and not to the sinners?

(7) In 2 Corinthians 8:4 Paul referred to the ministering to the saints as "the *fellowship* of ministering to the saints." Did this include his ministering to *sinners*? No, it did not include the ministering to sinners! He did not engage in the fellowship of ministering to sinners*!*

(8) In 2 Corinthians 9:13b Paul says: "...and for your liberal *distribution* unto them and unto all *men*." In Green's Literal Translation of the Bible it says: "...and the generosity of the *fellowship* toward them and toward all." In Young's Literal Translation of the Holy Bible we read: "...and *for* the liberality of the *fellowship* to them and to all." Question: Was the *fellowship* to the saints and to all sinners or was it limited to the saints? To saints, no doubt.

Now back to the question we asked earlier: To whom does the expression "unto them and unto *all*" refer in 2 Corinthians 9:13? In view of the facts that: (1) the collection or contribution was *raised for the saints*, (2) Paul and the other messengers of the churches took upon them the work of *ministering to the saints*, (3) Paul wanted others to pray that he would *be delivered* from *the unbelievers* (i.e., sinners) in Judea and that his service would *be accepted of the saints*, and, (4) the ministering *to the saints* involved *fellowship* with those that were helped, it is obvious to me that the expression "unto them and unto all" refers *to saints*! The context in which a word is used often determines its exact meaning. "Unto *them*" refers to *saints* (2 Cor. 9:12-13) but not to *all* saints. It refers specifically to "the poor saints at Jerusalem" (1 Cor. 16:1-3; Rom. 15:25-32). "Unto *all*" refers to *other saints* who in some way were helped or benefited by the collection or contribution. Since the word translated *distribution* in 2 Corinthians 9:13 is also translated *fellowship* in Green's and Young's Literal Translations, the *distribution* or *contribution* was in fact *fellowship* "unto them (the poor saints in Jerusalem) and unto all" (*other saints* who in some way benefited from that fellowship). If unbelievers, i.e., sinners, were the "all" under consideration, then sinners received fellowship as well as "saints at Jerusalem". Let us consider the fact that those relieved in 2 Corinthians 9:12-14 also offered "many thanksgivings unto God". They also *glorified God* and *prayed* for those who helped them! Does this sound like sinners? Let us keep in mind that the *distribution* was *fellowship* and Paul and others were engaged in "the *fellowship* of ministering to the saints". The "them" and the "all" were partakers of the *fellowship*. The *contribution* (fellowship) was proof of the love that Gentile Christians had for Jewish Christians. Did the churches extend fellowship to or have fellowship with unbelievers (sinners)? Should churches today extend fellowship to or have with fellowship unbelievers? Of course not.

Let us consider one other point on this passage. Since the collection was raised for saints, was sent to saints, and was received by saints and supplied the needs of saints, do you think that Paul would have misapplied it? Surely not.

1 Timothy 5:16
"If any man or woman that believeth have widows, let them relieve them, and let not the church be charged; that it may relieve them that are widows indeed." Note: A widow cannot "be taken into the number" unless she meets certain qualifications. For example, she must be "desolate" and one who "trusteth in God". For other qualifications see 1 Timothy 5:5-12. Without question, church benevolence is limited—even

among saints! I find no authority in the New Testament for churches, as such, to practice unlimited benevolence!

2 Thessalonians 3:10

"For even when we were with you, this we commanded you, that if any would not work, neither should he eat." The American Standard Version says: "...If any will not work, neither let him eat." Note: In view of this passage, it is evident that if a person is able to work, but he will not work, he should not be able to eat! The church, as such, has no responsibility to feed such a person even though he may claim to be a Christian. Yes, *church benevolence is limited*! Some, but not all, among the *saints* are objects of church benevolence.

Some Passages Used in an Effort to Prove That the Church Is Not Limited in its Benevolence

Most men that I know who believe in "church supported benevolent organizations" also believe in what is called "unlimited church benevolence" although they do restrict it in some cases. Among those who have advocated such are men like Tom Warren, Guy Woods, Roy Deaver, Alan Highers and others. In addition to 2 Corinthians 9:13 that I have already discussed, these men use such passages as Galatians 6:10; James 1:27; Matthew 5:44-48; 1 John 3:16-17; James 2:13-17 and Acts 20:35. There is no proof that any of these passages show *church* responsibility, but they do show *individual* responsibility. Let us consider these passages as time permits.

Galatians 6:10

"As we have therefore opportunity, let us do good unto all *men*, especially unto them who are of the household of faith." The argument is made that "all *men*" is another class of individuals in addition to "those who are of the household of faith." The truth is simply this. The "all *men*" of this verse includes "all *men*," some of which are of the household of faith. As we have opportunity we are to do good unto all men [both saint and sinner] and especially to those who are of the household of faith, i.e., saints. Yes, we, as Christians, have a general responsibility to do good unto all. This passage is showing *individual* responsibility and not congregational (i.e., church) responsibility as such.

The fact that the book of Galatians is addressed to "the churches of Galatia" [1:1] does not prove that Galatians 6:10 is church (congregational) responsibility. It says "As we have therefore opportunity, let us do good unto all men..." When Paul said "we" and "us" in this verse, was he speaking of *churches* or *Christians*? Let us consider the following. In Galatians 3:13 Paul said: "...Christ hath redeemed us...being made a curse for us..." Was he speaking of "us" churches or "us" Christians? We were redeemed as individuals and not as churches!

In Galatians 4:28 Paul said: "Now we, brethren...are the children of promise." Was Paul speaking of "we" churches of "we" Christians? Obviously he was not speaking of churches, but Christians as individuals! Christians are the children of promise.

We are told in Galatians 5:5 that "If we live in the Spirit, let us also walk in the Spirit." Was Paul speaking of "we" and "us" as churches or as Christians? No doubt, he was speaking of "we" and "us" as Christians and not as churches!

In Galatians 6:9 we read: "And let us not be weary in well doing: for in due season we shall reap, if we faint not." Was Paul speaking of "us" and "we" not being weary and fainting as churches or as Christians for we shall reap if we do not faint? Obviously, he was speaking of "us" and "we" as Christians and not as churches or congregations!

Let us notice again Galatians 6:10. It says: "As we have therefore opportunity, let us do good unto all *men*, especially unto them who are of the household of faith." Was Paul speaking of "we" and "us" as churches or "we" and "us" as individual Christians? Since "we" and "us" are plural pronouns, referring to persons or people, to whom do they refer? Do they refer to persons or people as individual Christians or do they refer to persons as groups, units or collectives as churches?

Let us now make this observation. Paul included himself in the pronouns "we" and "us". He said as "we" have opportunity, let "us" do good. Was Paul a church or was he a Christian? Paul was not saying, "As we (churches) have therefore opportunity, let us (churches) do good unto all men..." He was saying, "As we (Christians) have therefore opportunity, let us (Christians) do good unto all men..." In view of all the evidence, we must conclude that Galatians 6:10 gives us *individual* responsibility and not *church* responsibility.

James 1:27

"Pure religion and undefiled before God and the Father is this, To visit the fatherless and widows in their affliction, and to keep himself unspotted from the world." This passage is often used in an effort prove that churches may send contributions to "benevolent organizations" such as Childhaven and Home for the Aged. It is also used in effort to justify unlimited "<u>church</u> benevolence". First, let us look at James 1:27 in its context and see if it is *church* responsibility or *individual* responsibility being discussed.

Throughout the book of James, emphasis is placed on the individual. In James 1:5 we read: "If any of you lack wisdom, let *him* ask of God...and it shall be given *him*." Verse 6 says "But let *him* ask in faith..." Verse 12 says: "Blessed is the *man* that endureth temptations: for when *he* is tried, *he* shall receive a crown of life..." Verse 13 – "Let no *man* say when *he* is tempted, *I* am tempted of God..." Verse 14 – "But every *man* is tempted, when *he* is drawn away of *his* own lust, and enticed." Verse 18 – "Of his own will begat he us with the word of truth, that we should be a kind of firstfruits of his creatures." Note: The "us" and the "we" included James and other individuals. Verse 19 – "...let every *man* be swift to hear, slow to speak, slow to wrath." Verse 25 – "But whoso looketh into the perfect law of liberty, and continueth therein, *he* being not a forgetful hearer, but a doer of the work, this *man* shall be blessed in *his* deeds."

James 1:26 – "If any *man* among you seem to be religious, and bridleth not his tongue, but deceiveth *his* own heart, this *man's* religion is vain." James 1:27 appears in this context.

Individual, not *church,* responsibility is being shown.
James1:27 tells us that "Pure religion and undefiled before God
and the Father is this, to visit the fatherless and widows in
their affliction, and to keep himself unspotted from the world."
James is discussing a man's religion! He is not discussing
whether or not a church, acting in its congregational capacity,
can or should practice pure religion. James does not give the
whole or totality of what constitutes pure religion. He gives two
responsibilities that are involved and are essential in pure
religion. Verse 26 tells us that an unbridled tongue can make a
man's religion vain. We must conclude from this that bridling
the tongue is also involved in and essential to pure religion.
James 1:27 is telling us that the individual Christian is to
practice pure religion by visiting the fatherless and widows in
their affliction and keeping himself unspotted from the world.
We learn from verse 26 that a man must bridle his tongue and
not deceive his own heart in order to practice pure religion. We
may learn other responsibilities that we have from other
passages. They also may be involved in pure religion.

Matthew 5:44-48
"...Love your enemies, bless them that curse you, do good to
them that hate you, and pray for them which despitefully use
you, and persecute you; That ye may be the children of your
Father which is in heaven: for he maketh his sun to rise on the
evil and on the good, and sendeth rain on the just and on the
unjust. For if ye love them that love you, what reward have ye?
Do not even the publicans the same? And if ye salute your
brethren only, what do ye more than others? Do not even the
publicans so? Be ye therefore perfect, even as your Father
which is in heaven is perfect." Note: Jesus was giving
individual responsibility and not *church* responsibility. Of
course, we should love our enemies and do good to them that
hate us.

1 John 3:16-17
This passage shows *individual,* not *church,* responsibility. It
teaches that if we see a *brother* have need, we should have
compassion on him and help him. The responsibility shown
here is for *brethren.*

James 2:13-17
This passage teaches us that "If a brother or sister be naked, and destitute of daily food" our faith should work by providing the needs of that brother or sister. *Individual,* not *church,* responsibility is taught here and it is toward *brethren.*

Mark 14:7
"For ye have the poor with you always, and whensoever ye will ye may do them good: but me ye have not always." There is nothing in this verse [or context] to indicate *church* responsibility to the poor, [although *churches,* as such, in some cases do have the responsibility to help *some* saints].

Acts 20:35
"...It is more blessed to give than to receive." NOTE: This verse simply states a principle that is generally true, but does not show *church* responsibility!

Christians have a "benevolent" responsibility to both saints and sinners, but especially to Christians! *Churches* have a right to provide the needs of some saints, but not all – but not to alien sinners!

5

THE SPONSORING CHURCH

L. A. STAUFFER

Introduction

What the speakers at this conference say will have an unfamiliar sound to anyone who has no knowledge of the Restoration Movement, its validity, its controversies, and the terminology that has been employed to respond to beliefs and practices unknown to the scriptures. And much of what is said will seem trivial in a generation of disciples who have an agenda that is not primarily focused on a return to the practices of the church Jesus built. What will be said here is founded on the premise that the beliefs and practices of the first century church are of eternal significance. The soundness of the movement to return to first century Christianity depends on the truthfulness and scripturalness of a simple slogan: "We must speak where the Bible speaks and be silent where the Bible is silent." This principle raises the question: Do men need a "thus saith the Lord" for all that they teach in the name of the Lord?

Many brethren are scoffing at that notion and have moved, they believe, to "higher" and "nobler" principles of spirituality. They will find thoughts and arguments about sponsoring churches "narrow," "traditional," "ritualistic," "trivial," "unimportant," and "insignificant." What is said here is little more to them than "denominational doctrine" from the church of Christ. It is apparent in the thinking of some of these brethren that they have moved beyond the need of authority for every belief and practice and have arisen, in their opinion, to the high ground of deeper spirituality, the preeminence of sincerity, and tolerance and broad-minded acceptance of all men of faith.

But there must be, brethren, no apology for biblical teaching concerning the nature and character of the church Jesus established on that first Pentecost after His death, resurrection, and ascension to God's right hand. The work that the Lord assigned this body of believers and the organization by which it was to function is as essential to its existence among men as the plan of redemption that admits men into its fellowship. Discussions of gymnasiums and ball teams, human institutions and sponsoring churches, and social gospel goals and projects will among many brethren seem like minor issues of interest only to a few preachers and debaters. But in reality these controversies challenge the very fundamentals of New Testament Christianity and the Lord's church.

Brethren have learned in the two hundred or so years of the effort to restore "the ancient order of things" that rejecting one principle of Bible truth leads to the rejection of others. Those of past generations who rejected God's teaching concerning the work and organization of the church have rejected elements of the plan of salvation, basic moral principles, the distinctive identity of the Lord's church, and the very need for biblical authority itself. These words of warning are intended to prepare hearts for an open minded and serious examination of what the Bible teaches about "sponsoring churches."

Historical Perspective

Few issues have created the turmoil and division among believers in every generation of the Lord's church as God's plan for the independence and autonomy of local churches. Faithful brethren, fully committed to the authority of the Lord and His word, see wisdom in this design, but other brethren full of zeal and good intentions have for many reasons sought to bind or loosely join individual churches together in a variety of brotherhood arrangements.

This was true of believers early in the second century. Churches, according to the letters of Ignatius, elevated one elder above others in local churches and distinguished them with the term bishop. By mid-century metropolitan bishops oversaw bishops of all the congregations in entire cities, and in time patriarchs controlled the metropolitans of the cities in major regions of the empire. History details how this led to a universal bishop—the pope who in Rome became the head of the Roman Catholic Church. When men of the Reformation Era rejected and opposed the authority of the pope, sentiment was expressed for a return to the independence of local churches, but it was not until the early days of the Restoration Movement at the beginning of the nineteenth century that serious efforts were expended to focus on and highlight the organization and separateness of local congregations.

The very idea of "restoration" called for speaking where the Bible speaks and being silent where the Bible is silent, as framed in a sermon by Thomas Campbell in the summer of 1809 and taught by the apostle Peter (1 Pet. 4:11). Campbell's insistence that believers remove all the "rubbish of the ages," a reference to the traditions of men, and his call for a "thus saith the Lord" for every belief and practice brought early on a study and analysis of the organization of the first-century church. Alexander Campbell, Thomas' son, keyed in on this issue by the mid-1820s in a publication called *The Christian Baptist*.

Alexander Campbell, beginning in 1825, published a series of 32 articles entitled, "A Restoration of the Ancient Order of Things." In these articles he expressed in strong terms opposition to the "pretensions of the clergy," "the use of creeds as standards of orthodoxy," and "unauthorized organizations of the churches."[1] He spoke plainly: "The church is robbed of its character by every institution, merely human, that would ape its excellence and substitute itself in its place."[2]

It is startling how soon thereafter and how radically Alexander Campbell altered his view of human institutions and their value to the spread of the gospel. His thinking changed when through the influence of the so-called "new evangelism" of Walter Scott restoration churches began to grow rapidly. He even started a new paper in 1830, *The Millennial Harbinger*, to herald the need for greater cooperation among the churches to evangelize the world. He stressed the need for a "more efficient organization of the churches" and how "our present cooperative system is comparatively inefficient and inadequate" for the times and the cause for which they pleaded.[3] He stressed that a church can do what an individual cannot do and a "district of churches can do what a single congregation cannot."[4] After a couple of decades of this teaching, the influence of Campbell moved the majority of brethren to establish the American Christian Missionary Society in 1849 through which churches by their contributions began to cooperate in evangelism.

Within another generation brethren who had opposed the missionary society searched their minds and the scriptures for an alternate but "biblical" plan of cooperation among local churches. Brethren in Dallas, Texas, following the Civil War, urged churches to cooperate under the "sponsorship" of the elders of a single congregation to support preachers in destitute fields. In 1910 churches in west Tennessee proposed a similar effort under the "sponsorship" of the elders of the Henderson,

---

1 Winfred E. Garrison and Alfred T. DeGroot, *The Disciples of Christ, A* History (St. Louis: Christian Board of Publication, 1948), 176.

2 *The Christian Baptist*, Vol. I, p. 33

3 Earl Irvin West, *The Search for the Ancient Order* Vol. I (Nashville, TN: Gospel Advocate Company, 1949), 167.

4 L. A. McAllister, W. A. Tucker, *Journey in Faith: A History of the Christian Church (Disciples of Christ)* (St. Louis: Bethany Press, 1975), 168-169.

Tennessee church to evangelize that area of the state. Beyond these days a number of city-wide evangelistic efforts were proposed and supported by many churches under the "sponsorship" of a single congregation—notably Nashville, Tennessee and Houston, Texas. At the end of World War II congregations proposed and received funds from many churches to send and support preachers in war ravished nations overseas.

While this view of cooperation and approach to evangelism was common among churches of Christ up to the 1950s, there was never a time when brethren did not oppose such plans. Jacob Creath, Benjamin Franklin, a considerable number of brethren, and even congregations wrote in opposition to the Missionary Society from its inception. So it was of plans for churches to cooperate through a single congregation. David Lipscomb wrote of the West Tennessee plan of cooperation under a local eldership: "Now what was that but the organization of a society in the elders of the church? The church elders at Henderson constitute a board to collect and pay out the money and control the evangelists for the brethren in West Tennessee, and all preachers are the solicitors for this work. This very same course was pursued in Texas a number of years ago. The elders at Dallas were made the supervisors of the work, received the money, employed the preachers and directed and counseled them."[5]

In the early 1950s, the creation of a national radio and TV program of churches of Christ, called Herald of Truth, sparked the beginning of a generation-long controversy, study, and debates over the scripturalness of many churches cooperating through human organizations and through and under the oversight of the elders of local churches. Herald of Truth was sponsored by the Highland Avenue church in Abilene, Texas, was supported by funds from churches throughout the nation, and was under the oversight of the elders of that church. Benevolent institutions were also overseen by elders of local

---

5 Homer Hailey, *Attitudes and Consequences in the Restoration Movement* (Bowling Green, KY: Guardian of Truth Foundation, 2011), 253-254.

churches and supported with the funds contributed by other churches. These kinds of arrangements came to be called "sponsoring churches" and ignited a fresh interest in a study of the organization of the church Jesus built. Again, as in previous controversies, the call went forth for a "thus saith the Lord" for these practices. Discussions and debates tested the words of Thomas Campbell: "We speak where the Bible speaks and are silent where the Bible is silent."

Organization of the Church

"Sponsoring churches," as with "human institutions" supported by churches, can only be studied profitably against the backdrop of the organization of the first century church. The issue here, as with so many Bible subjects, is not the clarity of the scriptures, but whether man will accept what God has revealed. Luke tells us plainly that at the end of Paul's first preaching tour in Asia that he and Barnabas revisited the churches they had established and "appointed for them elders in every church" (Acts 14:23, ASV). These elders were called "bishops" or "overseers" and were commanded to "tend" or "shepherd" the "church of the Lord" (Acts 20:17, 28).

The apostle Peter, who himself was an elder, wrote to fellow elders and told them to "tend the flock of God *which is among you*, exercising the oversight" (1 Pet. 5:2). God's plan, thus, called for elders in every congregation and limited their oversight to the flock in which they were appointed. The flock itself was told to "know" them who labor and are "over" them "in the Lord." Brethren were also commanded to "obey" and to "submit" to them—"for they watch in behalf of your souls, as they that must give an account" (1 Thess. 5:12; Heb. 13:17). Elders, as men who lead and oversee their own households (1 Tim. 3:5), are to guide and direct the churches where they have been ordained bishops and shepherds. It is not a complicated arrangement.

These verses establish a number of unavoidable conclusions:

4. Every local church is independent of every other congregation. Elders of one church have no oversight or

control of another body of believers, including its members and its work.

5. Each local congregation under its eldership is autonomous, meaning that it is a self-governing body led by its elders under the authority of Jesus its head.

6. No eldership of a local church has authority to become an agency or medium of oversight through which other churches complete the work God has assigned to all local congregations equally.

How could any arrangement of these churches under the oversight of one of them not violate the biblical principle of "tending the flock which is among you"?

Cooperation: Biblical Examples

Proponents of sponsoring church programs respond to these truths by citing the biblical precedent of one church sending funds to another church. They point to the example of the brethren at Antioch when "the disciples, every man according to his ability, determined to send relief unto the brethren that dwell in Judea." And they did so by "sending it to the elders by the hands of Barnabas and Saul" (Acts 11:27-30). Here, it is noted, is an example of one church sending funds to another church. This shows, it is argued, that the independence and autonomy of a local church is not violated by the sending of funds from one church to another.

Advocates of this practice note also the command of Paul to the churches of Galatia and Corinth to take up a collection of funds to send to the needy saints at Jerusalem. The apostle wrote to Corinth: "Now concerning the collection for the saints, as I gave order to the churches of Galatia, so also do ye. Upon the first day of the week, let each one of you lay by him in store, as he may prosper, that no collections be made when I come. And when I arrive, whomsoever ye shall approve, them will I send with letters to carry your bounty unto Jerusalem" (1 Cor. 16:1-3).

Paul wrote a year later of this matter and urged the Corinthians out of their ability to complete their giving as a proof of their love so that he and the "messengers" selected by the churches can deliver this bounty to the needy saints at Jerusalem. In an important explanation of these gifts from the churches he writes: "For I say not this that others may be eased and ye distressed; but by equality: your abundance being a supply at this present time for *their* want, that their abundance also may become a supply for *your* want; that there may be equality; as it is written, He that gathers much had nothing over; and he that gathered little had no lack" (2 Cor. 8:13-15).

A number of vital truths and principles can be gleaned from these examples of churches cooperating with one another:

6. A church may send to another church to assist the receiving church to do its work of benevolence.

7. The sending churches helped the receiving church by sending it to the hands of the elders.

8. Churches may send the funds by the hands of messengers whom they themselves select to deliver the funds to the elders.

9. The funds are sent to the receiving church or churches to help them supply "their" want.

10. The church or churches sending funds are not authorized to supply any more than the "want" of the receiving church.

11. The elders of the Jerusalem church, in this case the receiving church, are not sponsoring a work for the contributing churches. They are overseeing the work and need of the flock among them.

Supporters of sponsoring church arrangements have made two arguments to counter these conclusions and to rationalize churches accomplishing God's work for many churches under the eldership of a single church. First, in the case of the Judean brethren (Acts 11:27-30), it is presumed that since Paul and Barnabas, after distributing funds to the elders for the needs of the saints in Judea, returned to Antioch from Jerusalem (Acts 12:25), they actually went only to Jerusalem and not to other churches in Judea. It is further assumed that they gave the money to the elders in Jerusalem and those elders made distribution to saints in all the churches of Judea as each church or man had need.

Clearly, it is a leap in logic to conclude that because the messengers returned from Jerusalem to Antioch they must have gone only to Jerusalem with this support. It may well be that Jerusalem was the last city of Judea that they visited with this relief. It could be that Jerusalem was the first city they visited and that they visited other cities in Judea and returned to Jerusalem before their departure to Antioch. Regardless of the specifics of the journey from Antioch to Jerusalem and Judea, it is clear that the principles of the independence and autonomy of local churches preclude the elders of Jerusalem having oversight of the work in other churches throughout Judea.

One of the great blunders in the controversy over sponsoring churches was made by brethren who attempted to combine the events of Acts 11 with the contribution Paul commanded of Corinth and the churches of Galatia (1 Cor. 16:1-3). Brethren affirmed that the contributions of the Corinthians and Galatians were sent to Jerusalem, but that, according to Acts 11, the need was in Judea. They then assumed that the funds were taken to the elders at Jerusalem (see Acts 21:17-18) and distribution was made by them to the churches and saints in Judea. The argument fails because the need of Acts 11 and the need of 1 Corinthians 16 are two different occasions separated by some 10 to 15 years.

Cooperation: Benevolence Versus Evangelism

It is apparent when churches send funds to another church for benevolence that the receiving church does not become a "sponsoring" church for the churches that send the relief. The receiving church is not functioning or sponsoring a work for the sending churches. Receiving churches in benevolence under the oversight of their own elders are doing "their" work (2 Cor. 8:14). And, as Paul said, if the situation should be reversed, the church in Jerusalem would be responsible to supply "your" want—the need of the brethren in Corinth (2 Cor. 8:14). This is a distinction brethren overlook when they draw a parallel between a church sending to another church for evangelism and a church sending to another church for benevolence. This, of course, changes if a local church establishes a benevolent institution, receives funds and needy saints from other churches, and oversees those funds and the benevolence of the contributing churches.

Congregations, however, who send relief for benevolence to a needy church are not equally related to the work being done by the receiving church. The "needs" of saints in a particular congregation is the work of that congregation. This fact is apparent in Paul's use of the expressions "their want" and "your want" when drawing a distinction between the work of the Jerusalem church and the work of the Corinthian church. In the work of benevolence the boundary of the work of a congregation is the members who have joined themselves together to serve and work under the oversight of a body of elders who have been appointed in that specific church. The boundary of the work of a congregation in evangelism is the entire world to which all churches, according to their abilities, are mutually and equally responsible to send preachers and support them.

Note that no church ever sent funds to another church for the support of a preacher or for the work of evangelism in general. The reason is not hard to grasp. All local churches are, as stated, "mutually and equally" related to the work of preaching the gospel to the world. That is why a church that receives funds from other churches to evangelize a city, a nation, or the whole world becomes a "sponsoring" church who under its elders oversees a work on behalf of all the contributing churches. Every church is obligated and responsible for this work, and yet it is being overseen by one of the elderships. The work of evangelism is not the exclusive work of the sending churches or the receiving churches.

Cooperation: Evangelism

That churches cooperated in the work of evangelism no one can deny. This is noted especially in the support that the apostle Paul received when he labored with the church at Corinth. He writes: "I robbed other churches, taking wages of them that I might minister unto you; and when I was present with you and was in want, I was not a burden on any man; for the brethren, when they came from Macedonia, supplied the measure of my want; and in everything I kept myself from being burdensome unto you, and so will I keep myself" (2 Cor. 11:8-9).

Note the absence of any reference to a sponsoring church for Paul's work at Corinth. *First*, it was Paul who "robbed" or received wages from the churches. *Second*, it was Paul's need— "my want"—that was being supplied. *Third*, as Guy N. Woods, a noted supporter of sponsoring churches, said when opposing the scripturalness of missionary societies, "the brethren simply raised money and sent it directly to Paul. This is the way it should be done today."[6] Brother Woods is correct and it should be noted that not only were funds not sent to a "society" to support Paul they were not sent to a "sponsoring church."

Earlier, before Paul came to Corinth, he referred to the support he received from the Philippian brethren. He wrote: "And ye yourselves also know, ye Philippians, that in the beginning of the gospel, when I departed from Macedonia, no church had fellowship with me in the matter of giving and receiving but ye only; for even in Thessalonica ye sent once and again unto my need" (Phil. 4:15-16).

A desperate effort has been made by some brethren to make Philippi a sponsoring church for the work that Paul did at Corinth when he received wages from many churches (2 Cor. 11:8). Brethren have argued that the terms "giving" and "receiving" are accounting terms and that the Philippian

---

6 *Cogdill-Woods Debate: A Discussion on what constitutes scriptural cooperation between churches of Christ* (Lufkin, TX: Gospel Guardian Company, 1958), 291.

church was a sponsoring church who received and dispersed funds from other churches to supply Paul's need at Corinth. Philippi, brethren have asserted, was the only church that "received" and "dispersed" funds, but that they received those funds from many churches. An effort was made to combine 2 Corinthians 11:8 with Philippians 4:15-16. It was assumed, without proof, that when many churches provided Paul's wages at Corinth they did so by sending funds to the Philippian church which received and dispersed those funds to supply Paul's need.

This argument has several problems.

1. Paul says that at Corinth he received wages from "churches," not just the church at Philippi.

2. Paul says that at the time of the support from Philippi, no other church had "fellowship" with him, except the church at Philippi.

3. The support he received from Philippi was given to him "when"—at the time—he left Macedonia, which was before he arrived at Corinth. The time of the support from Philippi at Thessalonica and Macedonia preceded the days at Corinth when Paul took wages from "churches"—plural.

4. The "receiving" of the funds was by Paul and the "giving" of the funds was by the Philippian church.

5. Beyond the time at Macedonia and Thessalonica, when Paul received support only from Philippi, other churches provided his wages after he traveled to Athens and then onto Corinth (see Acts 17:15-18:1; 2 Cor. 11:8-9).

Conclusion

This controversy arose, brethren, as so many others have, because brethren refuse to be silent where the Bible is silent. The principle that "silence authorizes nothing" has been the basis for nearly every division among brethren of the Restoration Movement. It was the issue in the debate over the missionary society, instrumental music in worship, benevolent societies, sponsoring churches, church support of colleges, and church support of recreational and social programs.

When God says nothing, nothing is authorized. God's will is only revealed to man in what He has spoken. The secret things of God belong only to Him—not to man. What belongs to man are "the things that are revealed" (Deut. 29:29). Man is, thus, forbidden to "add to" or "go beyond" what is written (Deut. 4:2; 2 John 9). When God said nothing about a descendant of the tribe of Judah being a priest under Moses' law that established the reason Jesus could not be a priest under that law. This is confirmed by the example of Uzziah who was of the tribe of Judah and was stricken with leprosy when he in arrogance presumed to enter the temple and burn the incense (see Heb. 7:13-14; 2 Chron. 26:16-23).

All the arguments and debates on sponsoring churches and the explanations of what's wrong with these arrangements could have been eliminated if brethren would have but accepted the simple truth: God says nothing about one local church sponsoring the work of other churches in evangelism, edification, and benevolence. Again, brethren, let us speak where the Bible speaks and be silent where the Bible is silent (see 1 Peter 4:11).

6

THE SOCIAL GOSPEL:
KITCHENS, RECREATION, ETC.

BILL HALL

Should churches of Christ include kitchens and dining areas in
their buildings? Had you asked this questions to preachers in
1937, the year of my birth, practically all would have replied
with an emphatic "No!" They would have said it is not the work
of the church to spend money on church dinners and social
activities. Most would have accepted "dinners on the ground,"
with food spread on rough tables erected by some of the
members under trees. Some would have even accepted having a
dinner in the hallway in the basement. They would have been
forceful, however, in their rejection of spending money from the
treasury for social activities.

In 1947 M. Norvel Young, while speaking on the lectureship of
Abilene Christian College, encouraged churches to build new
buildings, to build them in good locations, and to include in

their buildings, among other things, a large fellowship room and cooking facilities that would be near this large fellowship room. He followed that up with articles in some of the "brotherhood papers," lending his encouragement to the building of fellowship halls and kitchens.[1]

Young's exhortations were not well received initially. Considerable controversy followed, even in the more liberal arenas. I remember the first time I heard of a church of Christ including a fellowship hall in its building. It was around 1953. The church felt compelled to defend its actions, doing so by saying they were also using the room for a Bible class. It was difficult to find a kitchen and dining area in the building of a church of Christ in the 1950s.

As churches of Christ enjoyed rapid growth in the '60s and '70s, accompanied by more liberal attitudes, new buildings were required, and it became more and more common for churches to include kitchens and dining areas in their building plans. As they moved into the 21st century, even gymnasiums were being built by many of the churches. This movement resulted in considerable protest. The purpose of this study is to determine what the real issue was behind these protests.

WHAT WAS THE ISSUE?

First, we consider what the issue was not. The issue was not whether someone could eat something in a church building. Some said, "If these people are right a mother couldn't give her hungry baby a bottle of milk in the church building." Such statements grew out of a misunderstanding. Further, the issue was not whether the building was sacred. "I don't believe the building is sacred," was commonly heard. The building is built for spiritual purposes. If not, it has no right to exist. But it is recognized by all that the flooring, brick, roof, etc. are not sacred.

What then was the issue? The issue was this: Is there New

---

1 Hughes, Richard. *Reviving the Ancient Faith*. (Grand Rapids: William B. Eerdmans Publishing Company, 1996) 247.

Testament authority for the local church to plan and provide materially for social activities in its program of work?

Consider the question, "Is there New Testament authority?" The Bible teaches that we must have New Testament authority for all that we do in the Lord's work. "And whatever you do in word or deed, do all in the name of the Lord Jesus, giving thanks to God the Father through Him" (Col. 3:17). One cannot do anything in the Lord's name unless he has authorized it. For example, suppose someone is digging up my backyard with a backhoe. My wife, upset, asks him why he is doing it. "Bill Hall asked me to do it," he replies. That's fine if I authorized his doing the work, but if I didn't authorize it, he can't do it "in my name." So it is if we do anything "in the name of the Lord Jesus." Such action requires the Lord's authority.

Another scripture: "All scripture is given by inspiration of God, and is profitable for doctrine, for reproof, for correction, for instruction in righteousness, that the man of God may be complete, thoroughly equipped for every good work" (2 Tim. 3:16, 17). The scriptures furnish the man of God for every good work. Consequently, if a thing is a good work, it will be authorized by the scriptures. If it is not authorized by the scriptures, it is not a good work, no matter how good it may appear to be.

Jesus asked a good question concerning the baptism of John: "Where was it from? From heaven or from men? " (Matt. 21:25) We would do well to ask that question of any activity in which we are involved.

The issue is this, regarding churches planning and providing materially for social activities: Can it be done "in the name of the Lord?" Is it a good work clearly authorized by the scriptures? Did the practice originate from heaven or did it originate from men's thinking?

RESPONSIBILITIES GIVEN TO THE CHURCH

To further help us focus on the issue, we refer to a list of duties that the Lord has given His church to do, stated originally by

Franklin T. Puckett in the Arlington meeting of 1968.[2] We abbreviate.

1. The church is to provide for an assembly of the saints (Heb. 10:24,25; Acts 20:7). In keeping with this duty, most local churches provide a comfortable auditorium large enough for the whole church to come together in one place (1 Cor. 14:23). Where is the authority for the church to build suitable facilities for an assembly of the saints? It is found in the command to assemble.

2. In such an assembly the saints are to observe the Lord's supper on the first day of the week (Acts 20:7; 1 Cor. 11:17-34). The church therefore provides a table, plates for bread and cups for the fruit of the vine. In many cases the church actually provides the bread and the fruit of the vine The authority for these is found in the command to partake of the Lord's supper.

3. In this assembly the church is to sing (Eph. 5:19; Col. 3:16). So the church provides song books and arranges for someone to lead singing.

4. In the assembly they are to pray together (1 Cor. 14:15). So the church arranges for someone to lead in prayer.

5. The church is to preach and attend to the teaching of God's word (Acts 20:7; 1 Cor.14:26). That's why the church provides a pulpit area with a public address system and equipment for PowerPoint presentations. The church also provides classrooms. Where is the authority for classrooms? It is in the duty given the church by the Lord to teach His word.

6. In the assembly the church gives as they have been prospered (1 Cor. 16:2; 2 Cor. 9:7). So, there are baskets provided for taking up a collection.

---

2 Puckett, Franklin T. "Individual Action vs. Church Action." In *The Arlington Meeting*, comp. Cecil Willis. (Marion, Indiana: Cogdill Foundation, 1976) 159.

7. The church is to support the preaching of the gospel (Phil. 4:15-16; 2 Cor. 11:8-9). In keeping with this duty, the church provides financial support for local preaching and, as it has ability, for men who evangelize in other parts of the world. The church might provide tracts, correspondence courses, and other needful things for evangelism.

8. The church is to provide for the needs of certain destitute saints (Acts 4:34-35; 2 Cor. 8-9. So the church might provide food, housing, or whatever is needed for their care. This work would not be done under the oversight of an institutional board, but it could be done under the oversight of its own elders.

9. The church is to discipline those who walk in a disorderly manner (2 Thess. 3:6).

The issue under consideration in this study: Do we add a "number 10", i.e., plan and provide materially for social activities for its members? If the Lord has given this duty to the local church, then each church should provide a kitchen and dining area and whatever else would be useful for social activities. In fact, just as the church provides bread and fruit of the vine for the Lord's feast, the church could provide the food for these feasts — *if* it is the duty of the church to plan and provide materially for social activities. But if there is no authority for the church to plan and provide materially for social activities, there is no authority for the facilities for the unauthorized activity. This is the issue.

RESTROOMS AND WATER FOUNTAINS

Efforts have been made to justify the inclusion of kitchens and dining areas in the building, some serious, others not so serious. In the "not so serious" category was the effort to equate "fellowship halls" with restrooms and water fountains. The restroom argument received little attention, but an article about "Willie the Water Cooler" was published widely in church bulletins. According to the article, Willie the water cooler was concerned that since people had decided it was wrong to eat in the church building, they might decide it was wrong to drink in the building, and as a result he would lose his place in the building. Lynn Headrick "hit the nail on the head" when he said, "When we start planning socials around the water cooler, we will remove the water cooler." His statement brings us back to the issue: Is there New Testament authority for the local church to plan and provide materially for social activities in its program of work? Restrooms and water fountains have no connection with social activities.

LOVE FEASTS

A more serious argument was based on the love feasts of the Bible. "They are spots and blemishes, carousing in their own deceptions while they feast with you" (2 Pet. 2:13). "These are spots in your love feasts, while they feast with you without fear, serving only themselves " (Jude 12). It has been thought by some that these verses provide authority for churches' planning and providing materially for social activities. But considerable controversy exists as to what the love feasts were.[3] Albert Barnes in his commentary suggests that this was just a reference to the Lord's supper.[4] Clarke speaks of the wealthier members' giving feasts for the poorer members.[5] The point is this: We do not have enough information concerning love feasts—as to what they were or whether or not the church itself was even involved—to authorize the local church's building kitchens and dining areas to be used for social activities.

EDIFICATION

Some have tried to justify kitchens and dining areas under the general authority for edification. It is stated that by eating

---

3 Orr, James, ed. *The International Standard Bible Encyclopedia.* Vol. 1. (Grand Rapids: William B. Eerdmans, 1974) 69-70.

4 Barnes, Albert. "Comments on Jude." In *Barnes on the New Testament.* (Grand Rapids: Baker Book House, 1959) 397-398.

5 Clarke, Adam. *Clarke's Commentary.* Vol. 6. (Nashville, TN: Abingdon Press, 1977) 954.

together and enjoying one another's company Christians are brought closer together and experience greater unity in Christ. This may well be the strongest argument for "fellowship halls."

It is interesting, however, that edification in the scriptures is never linked to eating a common meal together. Edification is linked to worship (Heb. 10:24,25; 1 Cor. 14:26). It is linked to the Lord's giving apostles, prophets, evangelists, pastors and teachers to His church (Eph. 4:11-16). This passage in Ephesians contains possibly the fullest and most concise discussion of the work of edification. Absent is any mention of church dinners and social activities. Further, edification is linked to one's refraining from placing a stumbling-block before a brother (Rom. 14:19; 15:1,2; See also 1 Cor. 8:1). We do not offer this as a complete list of activities linked to edification, but there is no passage that links dinners and social activities to edification.

It is also interesting that many who accept kitchens and dining areas object to church owned gymnasiums. Why? If eating together promotes love and unity and edification, does not sharing in a basketball or volleyball game do the same? Why would one defend the first and object to the second?

Furthermore, the unity, the oneness, we have as brethren is founded upon our oneness with Jesus Christ, not on social activities we enjoy together (John 17:20-23); it is founded on one flock's looking to and following one Shepherd (John 10:16). A refusal to eat together may be a symptom of a lack of unity (Gal. 2:11-14), but eating together is not the true source of unity.

"Suppose the members pay for the facilities rather than taking the money from the treasury of the church?" someone might ask. In reply we would ask: Do the facilities then belong to the church? Is their use under the oversight of the elders? Is there really any difference in Christians' buying something and giving it to the church and their giving to the church that it might buy the same thing? In either case the church is placed in position of sponsoring social activities, a responsibility unauthorized by the Lord.

FELLOWSHIP

The argument we have heard most frequently for church kitchens and dining areas has been built on the word "fellowship." "Isn't the church to be involved in fellowship, and if so what would be wrong in the church's having a fellowship hall?" people have asked.

The Bible does teach that the church is to have fellowship, but we must understand the meaning of the word and its usage in the scriptures. The Greek word for fellowship is *koinonia*. The word is translated in various ways: fellowship, contribution, sharing, partnership, communion, etc. All of these words suggest the idea of joining together, so that we must ask, joining together in what? Sharing in what? Partnership in what? When many hear the word fellowship, their thoughts go to volleyball, hamburgers, cokes, or pot luck dinners. But is that what Bible fellowship points to?

Let's consider three possibilities: business, social, spiritual. Two men enter into a business partnership. It can be said of them that they are having "fellowship in business." People come together for a pot luck dinner, visiting and enjoying one another's company. It can be said that they are having "fellowship in social activities." People gather to pray together, sing and study the scriptures together. They are having "fellowship in spiritual activities."

Several questions need to be asked. Do the scriptures use the word fellowship in reference to a business partnership? Yes. "And so also were James and John the sons of Zebedee, who were *partners* with Simon" (Luke 5:10). James, John, and Simon Peter were having fellowship in the fishing business as suggested by the word "partners."

Do the scriptures use the word fellowship in reference to social activities? No. Not once. Isn't it amazing that people will use the word fellowship to try to justify the church's planning and providing materially for social activities when the scriptures never use the word in reference to social activities?

Do the scriptures use the word fellowship in reference to spiritual activities? Yes. The references are too many to list in this study. With the exception of Luke 5:10, mentioned above, the word *koinonia* is used in the scriptures of fellowship, sharing, communion, partnership, contribution in *spiritual activities* and *spiritual relationships.*

Fellowship in spiritual activities can be clearly seen in Philippians 4:15: "Now you Philippians know also that in the beginning of the gospel, when I departed from Macedonia, no church *shared* with me concerning giving and receiving, but you only. " See also Philippians 1:5. To see the negative use of the term, consider 1 Timothy 5:22: "Nor *share* in other people's sins. "

Fellowship in spiritual relationships can be clearly seen in 1 John 1:3: "That which we have seen and heard we declare to you, that you also may have *fellowship* with us; and truly our *fellowship* is with the Father and with His Son Jesus Christ. "

There is an interesting use of the word communion (fellowship) in 1 Corinthians 10:16: "The cup of blessing which we bless, is it not the *communion* of the blood of Christ? The bread which we break, is it not the communion of the body of Christ? " When we eat the bread of the Lord's supper we are having fellowship with the body of Christ. When we drink the cup we are having fellowship with the blood of Christ. Every church of Christ with which I am acquainted has a fellowship hall. It may be rented, owned by the church, or exist in someone's living room. It is the auditorium where Christians meet together to have fellowship in singing, praying, and worshiping God. The auditorium is the church's true fellowship hall. In that fellowship hall a meal is eaten. It is called the Lord's supper. This is the only meal that is associated with the word fellowship in the scriptures.

We know of only one scripture that would link a common meal to the activities of a local church — 1 Corinthians 11:17-34 — and Paul's response to their practice was negative. We are aware that some use this passage as "proof that the churches of the first century observed the Lord's supper after eating a meal together, and that Paul in this passage is just correcting the abuse growing out of the practice.[6] But Paul not only corrects the abuse, he commands that the practice of eating a meal cease: " What! Do you not have houses to eat and drink in? Or do you despise the church of God and shame those who have nothing? What shall I say to you? Shall I praise you in this? I do not praise you (1 Corinthians 11:22). Later he repeats himself, saying that if someone is hungry he should eat at home (1 Corinthians 11:34).

There is no evidence in scripture that the Christians of the first century, with approval from the apostles, accompanied their partaking of the Lord's supper with a common meal. Since the scriptures furnish us to every good work (2 Timothy 3:16, 17), any such accompaniment is not a good work and must be rejected by all who love truth.

In closing, we would ask this question: Do you really think that someone was reading the Bible in the 1960s or 1970s and came across a scripture that encouraged churches to plan and provide materially for social activities, and that the building of kitchens and dining areas resulted from this discovery? Or is it not more likely that churches of Christ followed the lead of the denominations, and having built their kitchens and dining areas, went to anything they could find to try to justify their unscriptural practice? We must reject whatever is not clearly authorized by scriptures that we might stand firmly on the truth of God's word.

---

6 Orr, James, ed. *The International Standard Bible Encyclopedia.* Vol. 1. (Grand Rapids: William B. Eerdmans, 1974) 69-70.